Mastering Reactive JavaScript

Create applications empowered with real-time data without compromising performance

Erich de Souza Oliveira

BIRMINGHAM - MUMBAI

Mastering Reactive JavaScript

First published: May 2017

Production reference: 1240517

Published by Packt Publishing Ltd.
Livery Place
35 Livery Street
Birmingham
B3 2PB, UK.
ISBN 978-1-78646-338-8

www.packtpub.com

Credits

Author
Erich de Souza Oliveira

Reviewer
Kevin Earley

Commissioning Editor
Amarabhab Banerjee

Acquisition Editor
Shweta Pant

Content Development Editor
Jason Pereira

Technical Editor
Leena Patil

Copy Editor
Safis Editing

Project Coordinator
Sheejal Shah

Proofreader
Safis Editing

Indexer
Francy Puthiry

Graphics
Jason Monterio

Production Coordinator
Shantanu Zagade

About the Author

Erich de Souza Oliveira is a developer with 10 years of experience, mostly in JavaScript, Scala, and Java. He has already worked for big companies and start-ups and currently works as a Chief Technology Officer for a brazilian video platform, called Winnin.

He is the author of Studio.js (microservices library for JavaScript) and can be found talking and attending South American conferences. He has a special interest in functional reactive programming, micro services, information retrieval, and recommender systems.

"I would like to give special thanks to my family and my girlfriend, for being so supportive throughout the writing of this book, Packt for the opportunity and for the amazing help they gave me with Shweta, Jason, and Leena and all editors of this book, and finally all my coworkers from Winnin for all the help and enthusiasm they had in this journey from the beginning. To write this book was a dream come true for me, and I hope you enjoy reading it as much as I enjoyed writing it."

About the Reviewer

Kevin Earley has always been passionate about technology. In high school, he picked up programming as a hobby. After high school, he entered the United States Air Force, where he was an electronic technician for about 9 years.

While in the USAF, he had multiple opportunities to program several utility applications for his shop. Later, Kevin left the USAF to begin a career in software development with his best friend, Mark Bowren.

Over the last 22 years, Kevin has worked for multiple companies across dozens of industries. Kevin has worked with many different technologies, but his primary expertise is with Microsoft products.

Among Kevin's skills and talents is writing, especially technical and factual writing. Over the years, Kevin has had many opportunities to write professionally--things such as technical manuals, tests, and some religious studies. His interest in writing is what brought Kevin to Packt. One day, when he retires, Kevin hopes to write a great deal more.

Kevin currently resides in Chicago, Illinois, with his three young children, Noelani, Eliana, and Matthew "Max" Alexander.

> *I'd like to thank the author of this book for writing such a wonderful and useful book. I would like to thank my children for supporting my writing projects and being so patient while "daddy has to work with his words."*

www.PacktPub.com

For support files and downloads related to your book, please visit `www.PacktPub.com`.

Did you know that Packt offers eBook versions of every book published, with PDF and ePub files available? You can upgrade to the eBook version at `www.PacktPub.com` and as a print book customer, you are entitled to a discount on the eBook copy. Get in touch with us at `service@packtpub.com` for more details.

At `www.PacktPub.com`, you can also read a collection of free technical articles, sign up for a range of free newsletters and receive exclusive discounts and offers on Packt books and eBooks.

`https://www.packtpub.com/mapt`

Get the most in-demand software skills with Mapt. Mapt gives you full access to all Packt books and video courses, as well as industry-leading tools to help you plan your personal development and advance your career.

Why subscribe?

- Fully searchable across every book published by Packt
- Copy and paste, print, and bookmark content
- On demand and accessible via a web browser

Customer Feedback

Thanks for purchasing this Packt book. At Packt, quality is at the heart of our editorial process. To help us improve, please leave us an honest review on this book's Amazon page at www.amazon.com/dp/1786463385.

If you'd like to join our team of regular reviewers, you can e-mail us at customerreviews@packtpub.com. We award our regular reviewers with free eBooks and videos in exchange for their valuable feedback. Help us be relentless in improving our products!

Table of Contents

Preface

Does creating a live application to handle thousands of sources of real-time data sound hard to you? No more. Teach yourself some reactive programming, and you will be able expand your boundaries, creating applications empowered with real-time data without compromising performance.

What this book covers

Chapter 1, *What Does Being Reactive Mean?*, explains the basics of reactive programming and how it compares with imperative programming, and also shows some example usage.

Chapter 2, *Reacting for the First Time*, covers the basics of event streams and operators using bacon.js.

Chapter 3, *A World Full of Change - Reactive Extensions to the Rescue*, in this chapter we explore the definitions and types of Observers and Observables.

Chapter 4, *Transforming Data - Map, Filter, and Reduce*, covers the most basic and important operators from functional reactive programming.

Chapter 5, *The World Changes Too Fast - Operators to Deal with Backpressure*, explains different techniques to mitigate the problem of receiving data faster than you can process it.

Chapter 6, *Too Many Sources? - Combining Observables*, teaches you to combine different sources of data to create new ones.

Chapter 7, *Something Is Wrong - Testing and Dealing with Errors*, explains how to deal with errors in observables and how to test programs using functional reactive programming.

Chapter 8, *More about Operators*, shows some important operators that did not fit into the previous chapters.

Chapter 9, *Composition*, explains what a transducer is and why you should use it.

Chapter 10, *A Real-Time Server*, builds the backend part of an web chat application used as an example of functional reactive programming.

Chapter 11, *A Real-Time Client*, builds the frontend part of an web chat application used as an example of functional reactive programming.

What you need for this book

All you need to follow this book is a computer with a version of Node greater than 6 installed. All software mentioned in this book is free of charge and can be downloaded from the Internet.

Who this book is for

This book is written for developers with basic JavaScript knowledge. We will use ES6 and functional reactive programming to create beautiful and readable applications. Here you will learn how to deal with an infinite stream of data (such as using tweets, stock info, or even chat messages) without ever compromising your system performance.

Conventions

In this book, you will find a number of styles of text that distinguish between different kinds of information. Here are some examples of these styles, and an explanation of their meaning.

Code words in text, folder names, filenames, file extensions, pathnames are shown as follows: Open the file `index.js`.

A block of code is set as follows:

```
function hello(){
 console.log("Hello World");
}
```

Any command-line input or output is written as follows:

```
npm install
```

New terms and **important words** are shown in bold. Words that you see on the screen, for example, in menus or dialog boxes, appear in the text like this: "In order to download new modules, we will go to **Files** | **Settings** | **Project Name** | **Project Interpreter**."

Warnings or important notes appear in a box like this.

 Tips and tricks appear like this.

Reader feedback

Feedback from our readers is always welcome. Let us know what you think about this book—what you liked or disliked. Reader feedback is important for us as it helps us develop titles that you will really get the most out of.

To send us general feedback, simply e-mail feedback@packtpub.com, and mention the book's title in the subject of your message.

If there is a topic that you have expertise in and you are interested in either writing or contributing to a book, see our author guide at www.packtpub.com/authors.

Customer support

Now that you are the proud owner of a Packt book, we have a number of things to help you to get the most from your purchase.

Downloading the example code

You can download the example code files for this book from your account at http://www.packtpub.com. If you purchased this book elsewhere, you can visit http://www.packtpub.com/support and register to have the files e-mailed directly to you.

You can download the code files by following these steps:

1. Log in or register to our website using your e-mail address and password.
2. Hover the mouse pointer on the **SUPPORT** tab at the top.
3. Click on **Code Downloads & Errata**.
4. Enter the name of the book in the **Search** box.
5. Select the book for which you're looking to download the code files.
6. Choose from the drop-down menu where you purchased this book from.
7. Click on **Code Download**.

Once the file is downloaded, please make sure that you unzip or extract the folder using the latest version of:

- WinRAR / 7-Zip for Windows
- Zipeg / iZip / UnRarX for Mac
- 7-Zip / PeaZip for Linux

The code bundle for the book is also hosted on GitHub at `https://github.com/PacktPublishing/Mastering-Reactive-JavaScript`. We also have other code bundles from our rich catalog of books and videos available at `https://github.com/PacktPublishing/`. Check them out!

Errata

Although we have taken every care to ensure the accuracy of our content, mistakes do happen. If you find a mistake in one of our books—maybe a mistake in the text or the code—we would be grateful if you could report this to us. By doing so, you can save other readers from frustration and help us improve subsequent versions of this book. If you find any errata, please report them by visiting `http://www.packtpub.com/submit-errata`, selecting your book, clicking on the **Errata Submission Form** link, and entering the details of your errata. Once your errata are verified, your submission will be accepted and the errata will be uploaded to our website or added to any list of existing errata under the Errata section of that title.

To view the previously submitted errata, go to `https://www.packtpub.com/books/content/support` and enter the name of the book in the search field. The required information will appear under the **Errata** section.

Piracy

Piracy of copyrighted material on the Internet is an ongoing problem across all media. At Packt, we take the protection of our copyright and licenses very seriously. If you come across any illegal copies of our works in any form on the Internet, please provide us with the location address or website name immediately so that we can pursue a remedy.

Please contact us at `copyright@packtpub.com` with a link to the suspected pirated material.

We appreciate your help in protecting our authors and our ability to bring you valuable content.

Questions

If you have a problem with any aspect of this book, you can contact us at `questions@packtpub.com`, and we will do our best to address the problem.

1
What Does Being Reactive Mean?

If you have bought this book, you have probably already heard about reactive programming (or even functional reactive programming). Nowadays, a lot of developers claim to use it in their own project; it is also easy to find posts on the Internet saying how amazing it is when compared with older paradigms. But, know you are doing a great job with the tools you have in your hands.

Learning a new programming paradigm is really hard. Most of the time you don't even know you needed it before you already mastered it, and you always have to ask yourself if this is really something that is worth the hours of studying or if it is just a new buzzword that all the cool kids are talking about, without adding real value to your programming skills.

Maybe you have tried reactive programming before, even used it in a small project or, like me, you just thought it wasn't worth a try, but for some reason you decided to give the paradigm an opportunity, (you are always thirsty for knowledge, I know, I was in your shoes a couple of years ago). It took me a lot of time to understand why I needed reactive programming and how to master it. I want to make sure that you have an easier path than I had.

This book will guide you through the reactive programming principles, and using a lot of examples, I will show you how to process and combine different sources of data or events to create astonishing live applications. In this first chapter, we are going to use the `bacon.js` library just to understand the basics and then we will go deeper with **Reactive Extensions (RxJS)**.

Before we dive into programming, you need to understand what reactive programming is and the problems it is designed to solve.

This chapter will cover the following points:

- Understanding what reactive programming is
- Comparison between reactive programming and imperative programming
- Knowing what problems reactive programming solves
- Installation of the tools needed throughout this book
- The first example of functional reactive programming will use a JavaScript library

The reactive paradigm

Reactive programming is a paradigm where the main focus is working with an asynchronous data flow. You may read many books and see throughout the Internet that the reactive paradigm is about propagation of changes or some technical explanation that only makes it harder to understand.

Imperative programming makes you describe the steps a computer must do to execute a task. In comparison, functional reactive programming gives you the constructs to propagate the changes so you can focus on what to do instead of how to do it.

This can be illustrated in a simple sum of two numbers. In imperative programming $a = b + c$ is evaluated only in that line of code, so if you change the value of b or c, it doesn't change the value of a. But in a reactive programming world, you can listen for the changes. Imagine the same sum in a Microsoft Excel spreadsheet, and every time you change the value of the column b (or c), it recalculates the value of a, so you are always propagating the change for the ones interested in those changes.

The truth is that you probably already use an asynchronous data flow every time you add a listener to a mouse click or a keystroke in a web page you pass as an argument to a function to react to that user input. So, a mouse click can be seen as a stream of events that you can observe and execute a function on when it happens. But this is only one usage of event streams.

Reactive programming takes this to the next level–using it you can listen and react to changes in anything creating a stream of events from it, so you can react to changes in a variable or property, database, user inputs, external sources, and so on. For example, you can see the changes of value in a stock as an event stream and use it to show your user when to buy or sell in real time. Another common example for external sources streams is your Twitter feed or your Facebook timeline. Also, functional reactive programming gives you the possibility to filter, map, combine, buffer, and do a lot more with your streams of data or events. So using the stock example, you can easily listen to different stocks using a **filter function** to get the ones worth buying and show to the user a real time list of them, as shown in the following diagram:

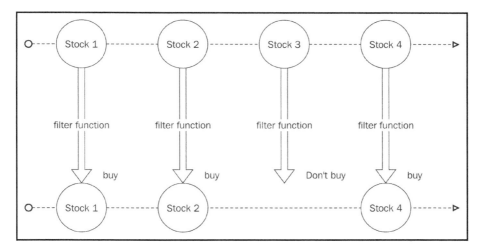

Why do I need it?

Functional reactive programming is especially useful when implementing one of these scenarios:

- Graphical user interface
- Animation
- Robotics
- Simulation
- Computer vision

A few years ago, all a user could do in a web app was fill a form with some data and post it to a server. Nowadays our web apps and mobile apps present to the user a richer interface, empowering them with real-time information and giving a lot more interaction possibilities. So, as the applications evolved, we needed more tools to achieve the new requirements.

Using it you can abstract the source of your data to the business logic of your application–this lets you write more concise and decoupled code, improves the reuse, and leads to a more testable code as you can easily mock your streams to test your business logic.

In this book we will use Reactive Extensions to explain and implement an example reactive application. Reactive Extensions are widely used in the industry and they have implementations for different languages (.Net, Scala, JavaScript, Ruby, Java, and so on) so you can easily translate the things you learn in this book to other languages.

In my personal opinion, Reactive Extensions have some concepts which are hard to understand for those unfamiliar with reactive programming. For this reason, we will learn the basics using a more simple library (`bacon.js`), and as soon as you understand the basics and the concepts, I will give you more tools using RxJS.

Installation of tools

Before we start to use reactive programming, we need to install the tools we will be using throughout this book.

Node.js

We will be using node version 6.9.1, the most recent LTS version of nodes at the time of writing. You can find versions of it for Windows, Mac, and Linux at the following link:

`https://nodejs.org/en/download/releases/`.

 We are going to use a lot of arrow functions throughout this book, so we expect you to have familiarity with this **ES6** feature. You can run the codes described here in any node version above 4.x.

bacon.js

In this first chapter of this book we will be using `bacon.js`, which is a library for functional reactive programming in JavaScript. This library works in both server and client. We will use it to introduce you to some concepts of functional reactive programming as it is easier to get started. We will be using version 0.7.88.

To install it on your server, just run the following command inside a node project:

```
npm i baconjs@0.7.88 -save
```

To add it to an HTML page, just paste the following code snippet inside it:

```
<script
src="https://cdnjs.cloudflare.com/ajax/libs/bacon.js/0.7.88/Bacon.min.js">
</script>
```

 Don't worry with the version not being above 1.x; bacon.js is stable.

RxJS

The last tool we need to follow in this book is RxJS; we will use this library in later chapters. This library also runs in both client and server and we will be using version 4.1.0.

To install it on your server, just run the following command inside a node project:

```
npm i rx@4.1.0 -save
```

To add it to an HTML page, just paste the following code snippet inside it:

```
<script src="https://cdnjs.cloudflare.com/ajax/libs/rxjs/4.1.0/rx.all.js">
</script>
```

 For those using other package managers, you can also install `bacon.js` and RxJS from Bower and NuGet.

Your first code using reactive programming

Now that you have installed all the tools we need to create our first program using functional reactive programming, we can start. For this first program we will be using bacon.js.

The bacon.js lets you work with events (which it calls **EventStream**) and dynamic values (which it calls **Property**). An EventStream represents a stream of events (or data), and it is an observable object where you can subscribe to be notified of new events on this stream. Bacon comes with a lot of built-in functions to create event streams from different sources such as button clicks, key strokes, interval, arrays, promises, and so on (and you can also create your own sources). A Property is an observable. Like an EventStream, the difference between both is that a Property has a current value. So every time you need to know of the changes and the current state of something, you will be using a Property; if you just want to be notified of the events and you don't need to know the current state of something, then you use an EventStream. A Property can be created from an EventStream using the `toProperty()` or `scan()` methods from the bacon.js API.

Like any other functional reactive programming, Bacon has a set of operators to let you work with your events, so you can map an event to something else, you can filter some events, you can buffer your events, you can merge different event sources, and a whole lot more.

We will be running our first example on Node.js, so let's get started:

1. Open your terminal and create a folder for this first project.
2. Now create a project:
     1. Navigate to the folder you have created.
     2. Type the following command:

        ```
        npm init
        ```

3. Keep hitting *Enter* to accept the default configuration.
4. If you did it right, you should see a message like this printed in your console:

    ```
    {
    "name": "example1",
    "version": "1.0.0",
    "description": "",
    "main": "index.js",
    "scripts": {
      "test": "echo \"Error: no test specified\" && exit 1"
    },
    ```

```
    "author": "",
    "license": "ISC",
    "dependencies": {}
}
```

OK, now we have our test project. In this project we will do a timer implementation–basically, what we want is to print the current time every second. We will do it with and without the functional reactive programming library, so first let's implement it in the traditional way.

Create a file called `traditionalInterval.js` and paste the following code inside it, and save:

```
setInterval(
    ()=> console.log(new Date())
,1000);
```

This code uses the function `setInterval ()` to call our function every `1000` milliseconds (every second). Now, run this program using the following command in your terminal:

node ./traditionalInterval.js

If you did it right it will print the current date every second in your terminal, like this:

```
2016-10-30T20:28:22.778Z
2016-10-30T20:28:23.796Z
2016-10-30T20:28:24.803Z
2016-10-30T20:28:25.808Z
2016-10-30T20:28:26.809Z
2016-10-30T20:28:27.815Z
2016-10-30T20:28:28.820Z
```

To stop your program just hit *Ctrl* + *C*.

Now let's see how we can implement the same program using bacon.js for functional reactive programming. First, we need to install `bacon.js` on our project, as described in the *Installation of tools* section and also described here:

npm i baconjs@0.7.88 –save

With `bacon.js` installed in our project we are ready to implement our program. First create a file called `baconInterval.js` and then, as we will require the library in our project, open this file in a text editor and paste the following code:

```
var Bacon = require("baconjs");
```

Now that we have added Bacon to our code, we can use it to create a timer that prints the current time every second.

Before showing you the code that does this, it's important to understand how we model this problem using functional reactive programming. As we described before, bacon.js implements the concept of event streams, which are an observable stream of events. To create a timer, we need a special type of stream, capable of emitting events every *x* seconds, so we can listen to this stream to print the current date.

The bacon.js has a lot of built-in functions to create EventStreams from different sources. We will discuss the available functions later, but at this time we need to know the `Bacon.interval()` function that lets us create an EventStreams that emits an event every *x* seconds, where *x* is the time between the events in milliseconds. So, if we want to send an event every second, we must use it as follows:

```
Bacon.interval(1000);
```

This code creates an EventStream that emits an event every second. Now we need a way to be notified of the events in this stream so we can print the current date on the console. We can do this using the `onValue()` function–this function lets us subscribe to listen to events on this stream, and it receives the function to be executed as a parameter, so it lets us change our code to use it. The full code is as follows:

```
var Bacon = require("baconjs");
Bacon
  .interval(1000)
  .onValue(
      ()=> console.log(new Date())
);
```

If you run this code, you will see an output like this:

```
2016-10-30T20:28:22.778Z
2016-10-30T20:28:23.796Z
2016-10-30T20:28:24.803Z
2016-10-30T20:28:25.808Z
2016-10-30T20:28:26.809Z
2016-10-30T20:28:27.815Z
2016-10-30T20:28:28.820Z
```

You still have to hit *Ctrl* + *C* to stop your program.

Here we are creating an EventStream from an interval. bacon.js has a lot of built-in methods to create event streams; we will see these methods in more detail in Chapter 2, *Reacting for the First Time.*

Congratulations, you have just created your first program using functional reactive programming Now, let's change it a little.

We are going to implement the same code, but using a `frp` operator. To do this we will use the `map ()` operator–this operator receives a mapping function as a parameter. This function takes an input value and transforms it in another value. Instead of listening to events on the stream and printing the current date on the console, we will listen to events in the stream, map those events to the current date, and then print the result. Create a file called `baconIntervalMap.js` and paste the following code:

```
var Bacon = require("baconjs");
Bacon
  .interval(1000)
  .map(()=>new Date())
  .onValue((currentDate)=>console.log(currentDate));
```

 Using the `map ()` operator we can write a more descriptive code. This also enables us to decouple our code and test each function, instead of the whole code. We will see the `map ()` operator in more detail in Chapter 4, *Transforming data - Map, Filter, and Reduce.*

If you run this code, you will see the same kind of output as from the previous code.

In the first example (without bacon.js) we have a hard code to test, because all logic of the code is tied together. In the next example, we improved our code testability, as we detached the source of the events from the action, so we can test our `onValue()` function mocking our EventStream, but the logic of getting the current date is still tied to the action (printing on the console). The last example (using `map()`) is a lot more testable, as we can test every single piece of code separately.

Let's see the last version of our problem. Instead of printing the current date every second forever, we will print the current date only five times, every second. We can implement it without using `frp` ; create a file called `traditionalInterval5times.js` and paste the following code:

```
var count = 0;

var intervalId = setInterval(()=>{
    console.log(new Date());
```

```
        count++;
        if(count===5){
            clearInterval(intervalId);
    }
},1000);
```

Now our code has become a lot more complicated. To implement the new version of the proposed code we need an external counter (to make sure we run the code only five times), and we need a reference for the interval scheduler so we can stop it later. By looking at this code it is not easy to understand what it is trying to do, and as you probably already noted, it is really hard to test.

You might be wondering how we can change our last `frp` code to implement; it would be amazing if we had a way to only listen to five events on our Bacons EventStream, so I present to you the `take()` method. This method lets you listen to only a given number of events on an EventStream. So, changing our previous code to run only five times is really straightforward; create a file named `baconIntervalMap5times.js` and paste the following code:

```
var Bacon = require("baconjs");

Bacon
    .interval(1000)
    .take(5)
    .map(()=>new Date())
.onValue((currentDate)=>console.log(currentDate));
```

 The `take()` operator lets us listen to only the first *x* events on the EventStream. We will see this operator in more detail in Chapter 8, *What Else? - More Operators*.

Our new code is that simple. We don't need to change the stream source, the mapping function, nor the subscription function; we just need to take only five events from the stream.

In this final example, we can see how functional reactive programming can improve our code readability. In the code using `setInterval()`, we had to add a counter variable to make sure we ran the log function the right number of times. We also had to remember to clear the interval so we didn't run this code forever. On the other hand, on the code using `frp` all we had to do was describe the transformations using `take()` to show how many items we wanted, `map()` to get the current date, and finally subscribed to react to the events of this stream.

If things are going too fast for you, don't worry–I just wanted to get your hands dirty with some `frp` code. In the following chapters we will see these concepts in a lot more detail.

Summary

In this chapter, we learned what functional reactive programming is and how it compares with imperative programming. We also learned where it comes from and modeled and implemented our first functional reactive program using the `bacon.js` library. We compared it with a program with and without `frp` and saw how it can improve our code maintainability and testability by separating the source of the events from the actions caused by them.

In the next chapter, we will take a more in-depth look into the `bacon.js` library, and what we can do with event streams, and we will also start to model and implement more complex examples using new operators.

2
Reacting for the First Time

In the previous chapter, you started understanding the motivations behind using functional reactive programming in your systems; you also saw how a program using this paradigm fared against a program without it. You learned how reactive programming can improve code readability and testability by decoupling your event sources from the action you take when the action occurs.

We started with some basic examples using `bacon.js` as the reactive programming library for JavaScript. In the examples, we began with creating our first EventStream from an interval. Then we started using some operators (`map()` and `take()`). Finally, we subscribed to this event source to take actions in the case of an event occurrence. This was just a kind introduction to functional reactive programming.

When reading most of the functional reactive programming libraries (for any language), you will see a lot of diagrams explaining how the operator works. In the previous chapter, I presented the following diagram to illustrate a **filter function**:

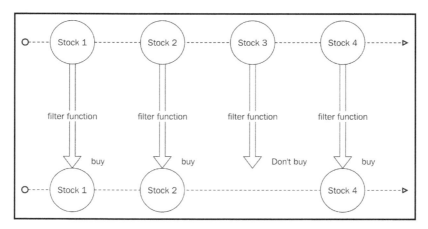

We will cover what this illustration means in detail in this chapter. Learning how to read this will make reading documentation on libraries a lot easier.

Functional reactive programming is a paradigm which is hard to master, so after the quick introduction, you'll now move on to learning how to implement more complex programs using the `bacon.js` library.

This chapter will cover the following points:

- Understanding bacon.js observable objects (EventStream and Property) and their differences
- Modeling a functional reactive program
- Subscribing to an observable
- Unsubscribing from an observable
- Reading a reactive programming operator diagram
- Using operators to transform an observable

The bacon.js observables

In functional reactive programming, an observable is an object where you can listen for events. This way, you can, for instance, create an observable for a button and then listen and act when a click happens.

The bacon.js gives you two flavors of an observable: the first one is EventStream and the other is Property. We will see the difference between the two objects later. To listen to events in an observable (or subscribe to an observable), you can use the `onValue()` method with a callback. So if you want to log every event in an EventStream, you can use the following code:

```
myEventStream.onValue(function(event){
    console.log(event);
});
```

 We will see how to create an EventStream in more detail later.

As we saw in the example in the last chapter, we can transform our observable using bacon.js operators. These operators let us filter, combine, map, buffer, and do a lot of other interesting things with our EventStream.

An observable can either finish or stay open to propagate events forever; it can also contain (and propagate) errors. We will see this in more detail later.

Creating our first observable

The bacon.js gives us a multitude of methods to create observables. We can create them from DOM events, promises, interval, and so on. Sometimes we might need to create an observable from our own source, so let's learn how to create our own event streams.

Observables from DOM events (asEventStream)

To create an EventStream from DOM events (a mouse click for instance), we will need an HTML page with jQuery (or **Zepto.js**); bacon.js adds the asEventStream() method for all jQuery objects. So if we want to create an EventStream from a button click, we can use the following code:

```
var clickEventStream = $('#myButton').asEventStream('click');
```

This line creates an EventStream from button clicks on a DOM object with the ID myButton. If we want to execute an action every time this button is clicked, we will need to use the onValue() method from this event stream. The following code shows an alert on the screen every time the user clicks on the button:

```
clickEventStream.onValue(function(){
    alert('Button clicked');
});
```

This code adds a function to be called every time an event happens in this EventStream object, as it emits an event every time myButton is clicked. The following code will show an alert every time this button is clicked.

As this is your first HTML code, I will paste the full HTML here so you can create a file with it and test it in your own browser:

```html
<html>
  <head></head>
  <body>
    <button id="myButton">CLICK</button>
    <script
src="https://cdnjs.cloudflare.com/ajax/libs/jquery/3.1.1/jquery.min.js"></s
cript>
    <script
src="https://cdnjs.cloudflare.com/ajax/libs/bacon.js/0.7.88/Bacon.min.js"><
/script>
    <script>
      var clickEventStream = $('#myButton').asEventStream('click');
      clickEventStream.onValue(function(){
        alert('Button clicked');
      });
    </script>
  </body>
</html>
```

Observables from promises (fromPromise)

You can also create EventStreams from ES6 promises or jQuery AJAX. These streams will contain only a single value (or an error in case of failure), and finish. We will need a promise to test this method:

```
var promiseObject = Promise.resolve(10);
```

Here, we are creating a successful promise that will return the value 10. To transform this promise into an EventStream, we use the following code:

```
Bacon
  .fromPromise(promiseObject);
```

 Keep in mind you will need Node.js version 4 or above, or a modern browser to test this code (old browsers don't have promises implemented).

Observable node event emitter (fromEvent)

Lots of Node.js modules implement an event emitter, which is basically an object with the `on()` method that is called every time an event happens. We can transform these objects into EventStreams of bacon.js to take advantage of all the transformations. The method `fromEvent()` has the following signature:

```
Bacon
    .fromEvent(eventEmitter,eventName);
```

The parameters are `eventEmitter`; the node `eventEmitter` object; and `eventName`, the name of the event. We can use the `fs` module to show the usage of this method.

To read a file using the `fs` node module that uses an event emitter, we need to create a `readStream` for the file using the following code:

```
var fs = require('fs');
var FILE_PATH = 'SOME FILE';
var readStream = fs.createReadStream(FILE_PATH,'utf8');
```

Then, subscribe to the events on this emitter using the `on()` method, as follows:

```
readStream.on('data', (content)=>console.log(content));
```

To transform this code into a code using a bacon.js EventStream, we need to change the last line of the following code:

```
var eventStream = Bacon.fromEvent(readStream,'data');
eventStream
    .onValue((content)=> console.log(content));
```

So comparing with the method signature, our `eventEmitter` parameter is the `readStream` object and `eventName` is `data`.

The `fromEvent()` method can also be used to listen to DOM events (similar to the `asEventStream()` method), as you can see in the following code:

```
var clickEventStream =
Bacon.fromEvent(document.getElementById('#myButton'), 'click');
```

Observables from an array (fromArray)

To create an observable from an array, you can use the `fromArray()` method, as shown in the following code:

```
var myArray = [1,2,3];
Bacon
    .fromArray(myArray);
```

Observables from an array (sequentially)

To create an observable from an array with a given interval to deliver each item from the array, we can use the `sequentially()` method, as follows:

```
var myArray = [1,2,3];
var intervalBetweenItens = 100;
Bacon
    .sequentially(intervalBetweenItens ,myArray);
```

This code emits the itens of the array with `100` milliseconds of interval between each emission.

Observables from an interval (interval)

We can create an observable from an interval; this is especially useful if you wish to execute repetitive tasks, and it can be used as a substitution for the `setInterval()` method. An EventStream created by the `interval()` method will never end; this method has the following signature:

```
Bacon.interval(intervalInMilliseconds);
```

It receives only one parameter, that is the interval between the events in milliseconds, and it will emit an empty object as the event. Let's say you have run the following code:

```
Bacon
    .interval(100)
    .onValue((event)=>{
        console.log(event);
    });
```

If so, you will see the following output:

```
{}
{}
{}
{}
```

It will keep printing an empty object until you kill the program.

Observables from other sources

The bacon.js has other built-in methods to create observables from common EventStream sources. The objective of this chapter is not to explain all the functions of the bacon.js API. You can check out other possible EventStream sources by referring to bacon.js documentation. The last important method to create an EventStream is the method that lets you create an EventStream from any arbitrary source. This is the `fromBinder()` method.

The `fromBinder()` method has the following signature:

```
Bacon.fromBinder(publisher);
```

It receives a `publisher` function as a parameter; this is a function with only one parameter that lets you push events for your EventStream, as illustrated in the following example:

```
var myCustomEventStream = Bacon.fromBinder(function(push){
    push('some value');
    push(new Bacon.End());
});
```

The following code creates an EventStream that emits a string and then finishes the EventStream. As you can see, `Bacon.End()` is a special object that tells bacon.js when to close the EventStream.

The following example sends more events to the EventStream and prints them to the console:

```
var myCustomEventStream = Bacon.fromBinder(function(push){
    push('some value');
    push('other value');
    push('Now the stream will finish');
    push(new Bacon.End());
});
myCustomEventStream
    .onValue((value)=>
        console.log(value)
    );
```

If you run this code, you should see the following output:

```
some value
other value
Now the stream will finish
```

When we want to propagate an error on our observable, we need to use the `Bacon.Error()` type to wrap the error. The bacon.js is not capable of automatically encapsulating a thrown exception; you always need to encapsulate it manually. It is also important to notice that when an error occurs, bacon.js doesn't end your observable (but you can configure it). Let's change the previous code to add an error as follows:

```
var myCustomEventStream = Bacon.fromBinder(function(push){
    push('some value');
    push('other value');
    push(new Bacon.Error('NOW AN ERROR HAPPENED'));
    push('Now the stream will finish');
    push(new Bacon.End());
});
myCustomEventStream
    .onValue((value)=>
        console.log(value)
    );
```

It will give you the same output and ignore your error, as you haven't added a handler for errors in this observable (we will see later how to add a handler using the `onError()` method). But if we want to finish the observable as soon as an error happens, we can call the `endOnError()` method to our observable, as you can see in this code:

```
var myCustomEventStream = Bacon.fromBinder(function(push){
    push('some value');
    push('other value');
    push(new Bacon.Error('NOW AN ERROR HAPPENED'));
    push('Now the stream will finish');
    push(new Bacon.End());
}).endOnError();
myCustomEventStream
    .onValue((value)=>
        console.log(value)
    );
```

It will give you the following output:

```
some value
other value
```

> As you can see, it never prints `Now the stream will finish` because the error happened before it.

Properties

Now you know what an EventStream is and how to create it; as discussed, it is an observable. However, bacon.js has another special form of observable called Property. A Property is an EventStream with the concept of current value. You can create a Property from any EventStream using the `toProperty()` or `scan()` method; it is especially useful to represent DOM data binding.

To create a Property from an EventStream, you can use the `toProperty()` method that has the following signature:

```
eventStream.toProperty(initialValue);
```

The `initialValue` parameter is optional. If you decide to omit it, you will have a Property without an initial value. If you pass it, it will be used as the current value of this Property until the first value is emitted from the stream.

The other way to create a Property is using the `scan()` method. This method is similar to the `reduce()` method from the JavaScript array object. Given a seed object and accumulator function, the `scan()` method will iterate over your EventStream to create a Property from the result:

```
Bacon
    .sequentially(100,['a','b','c','d'])
    .scan('=> ',(acc,b)=> acc+b)
    .onValue((value)=>console.log(value));
```

In this example, we first create an EventStream from an array of strings, then we call the `scan()` method to create a Property with a seed value of `=>`, and using a function to concatenate these value, we print the result to the console for each scan iteration. So running this code will give the following output:

```
=>
=> a
=> ab
=> abc
=> abcd
```

Changes in an observable

In the last section, we saw how to use the `scan()` method to create a Property from an EventStream. When we use this method (actually, when we use any operator), we do not change the original observable; we always create a new observable. So, it never interferes with the other subscriptions (and transformations) of the observable. We can change the previous code to listen to events on both the EventStream and the Property; now we will see that making changes in one of these two doesn't affect the other:

```
var eventStream = Bacon
    .sequentially(100,['a','b','c','d']);

eventStream.onValue((value)=>{
    console.log('From the eventStream :'+value);
});

var property = eventStream.scan('=> ',(acc,b)=> acc+b);

property.onValue((value)=>{
    console.log('From the property :'+value);
});
```

It gives the following output:

```
From the property :=>
From the eventStream :a
From the property :=> a
From the eventStream :b
From the property :=> ab
From the eventStream :c
From the property :=> abc
From the eventStream :d
From the property :=> abcd
```

This shows that the usage of the `scan()` method to concatenate the array in the Property does not change the behavior of the original `eventStream`.

Reacting to changes

As discussed earlier, an observable is an object where you can listen to events. The act of listening to events in this object is called **subscription**. Here, we will see the different ways in which we can subscribe to an observable and also how we can stop listening to events in this observable (unsubscribe).

Subscribing

We call subscribing to an observable an act of adding a function to be called when an event happens. Using bacon.js, we can be notified when a value is emitted (the onValue(), log(), and assign() methods), when an error has occurred (the onError() method), or when our observable is closed (at the end).

Subscribing using the onValue() method

The most common way of subscribing to an observable is using the onValue() method. This method has the following signature:

```
observable.onValue(functionToBeCalledWhenAnEventOccurs);
```

So let's subscribe to eventStream to log every event on this stream, as follows:

```
Bacon
    .fromArray([1,2,3,4,5])
    .onValue((number)=>console.log(number));
```

This code gives you the following output to the console:

```
1
2
3
4
5
```

This function can be used for any type of observable (EventStream and Property). The only difference is that in Properties, if the initial value of the Property exists, then it triggers the `onValue()` function. Check out the following code:

```
var initialValue =0;
Bacon
    .fromArray([1,2,3,4,5])
    .toProperty(initialValue)
    .onValue((number)=>console.log(number));
```

This will give you the following output:

```
0
1
2
3
4
5
```

When subscribing to an observable, it's important you know a way to unsubscribe it as well. The `onValue()` method returns a function; this function when called will unsubscribe your function from this observable. So we can create an observable from an interval and print a message every time an event is propagated, as follows:

```
Bacon
    .interval(1000)
    .onValue(()=>(console.log("event happened")));
```

It will print the message `event happened` every second until we kill the process. But if we want, we can use the return of `onValue()` to unsubscribe from our observable after a certain amount of time, as follows:

```
var unsubscribe = Bacon
        .interval(1000)
        .onValue(()=>(console.log("event happened")));

setTimeout(function(){
    console.log("unsubscribing")
    unsubscribe();
},4000);
```

With this code, the program will unsubscribe from your observable. This way, it exits normally and prints the following output:

```
event happened
event happened
event happened
unsubscribing
```

Subscribing using the log method

So far, every time we created an observable, we used the `onValue()` method to listen to events in the observable. In our examples, we usually just printed the value to the console, as this is common usage when testing observables and operators bacon.js has a special method through which you can print all the events to the console. All observables have the `log()` method. This method prints every event to the console and prints the `<end>` string when the event stream finishes. We can use it with EventStreams:

```
Bacon
    .fromArray([1,2,3,4,5])
    .log();
```

This code gives you the following output to the console:

```
1
2
3
4
5
<end>
```

As you can see, after all the events, it will print the `<end>` string to indicate the end of the EventStream. If we decide to use it with an infinite stream (a stream created with the `interval()` method), it will never print the `<end>` string (as you should expect). Refer to the following code:

```
Bacon
    .interval(100)
    .log()
```

This will print the following output:

```
{}
{}
{}
{}
```

It will keep on printing until you close the program.

We can also use the `log()` method with a Property, as you can see in the following example:

```
var stringProperty = Bacon
        .fromArray(['a','b','c','d'])
        .scan('=> ',(acc,b)=> acc+b);

stringProperty.log();
```

This will print the following output:

```
=>
=> a
=> ab
=> abc
=> abcd
<end>
```

As you can see, this prints the `<end>` string for a Property as well.

The `log()` method is especially useful for debug purposes and to test and see how an operator works. It is the fastest way to see an operator in action.

Subscribing using the assign method

The `assign()` method lets you call a function on an object every time an event occurs. It is especially useful to set the content of DOM elements. You can use it to set the value of a DOM object class using jQuery:

```
observable
    .assign($("#myElement"), "class");
```

The `assign()` method is just a synonym for the `onValue()` method.

Acting when an error occurs

In the previous sections, we saw how to encapsulate an error on bacon.js. Now, we will use the `OnError()` method to take an action whenever this happens. This method has the same signature as that of the `onValue()` method and works similarly, but only for bacon errors. Now with this method, we can change the code we used in the previous section to print an error when it occurs. This is shown as follows:

```
var myCustomEventStream = Bacon.fromBinder(function(push){
    push('some value');
    push('other value');
    push(new Bacon.Error('NOW AN ERROR HAPPENED'));
    push('Now the stream will finish');
    push(new Bacon.End());
});
myCustomEventStream
    .onError((value)=>
        console.log(value)
    );
```

It will print the following:

NOW AN ERROR HAPPENED

As you might expect, the `OnError()` method also returns a function to unsubscribe.

Reading how an operator works

Throughout this book, you will see a lot of diagrams explaining how an operator works. These diagrams are a graphical representation of observables and operations in those observables. Usually, the diagrams consist of three parts. On the top they shows a line with balls representing the initial state of an observable. The line itself represents an observable. The circles are events that happened in this observable and they are pushed from left to right; therefore, the leftmost ball is the first event, the second one is the second, and so on. This is illustrated in the following diagram:

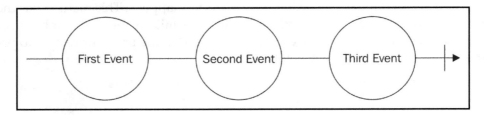

So, the preceding line represents an observable with three emitted events. The string at the center of each circle is the value emitted by that event. The short vertical line on the right-hand side of the diagram represents the end of this observable. This diagram is a graphical representation of the following observable:

```
Bacon
    .fromArray([
        'First Event',
        'Second Event',
        'Third Event'
    ]);
```

As we know, an observable can exist forever (the ones created using the `Bacon.interval()` method). To represent this kind of observable, we remove the short line on the right-hand side. This way, we show that other events might happen in this observable in the future, but we are not interested in them, , as shown in the following diagram:

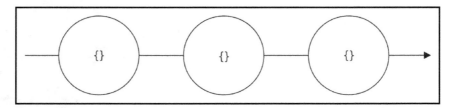

This diagram is a possible representation of the following observable:

```
Bacon
    .interval(1000);
```

Keep in mind, the time between events is irrelevant in this case, so we decided to omit it from the graphical representation (we usually omit this information, as this is an implementation detail). The `Bacon.interval()` method always emits an empty object, and for this reason, we draw brackets at the center of each circle.

The main reason for using this graphical representation is to show how an operator transforms an observable. So to show which operator is being used, we add an arrow pointing downward with the name of the operator and the content of the operator if needed. So if we want to represent the use of the `map()` operator, we can use the following diagram:

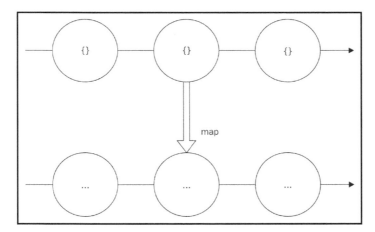

As discussed before, when an operator is applied to an observable, it creates a new observable (it does not change the original observable). For this reason, we add a new line that represents the new observable created after the operation. On this new line, I decided to omit the value at the center of the circle (adding only three dots), because the way the `map()` operator works is out of the scope of this discussion.

Sometimes we want to represent multiple operators. In such cases, we just keep chaining more lines. Some operators let you work with multiple observables, which makes the diagram more complex. But don't worry, we will explain the changes the first time they happen.

Transforming events using bacon.js

One important thing when learning functional reactive programming is how you can transform the events emitted by an observable. This way, you can use successive function calls to create new objects from the original input. This also improves the reuse of your code; every transformation of an observable creates a new observable, and each observable can have several listeners subscribed to it.

Before applying any transformations to our observables, let's implement an observable to generate and print the current date. To do this, let's use the `Bacon.interval()` method. So, the following code will emit an empty object every second:

```
var eventSource = Bacon
    .interval(1000);
```

Remember, `Bacon.interval()` emits an empty object every x milliseconds, where x is the argument passed to the function–in our example, every `1000` milliseconds, which is the same as every second.

Now we can just subscribe a function to print the current date to the console. We can do this using the `onValue()` function by adding the following line:

```
eventSource
    .onValue(()=>{
        console.log(new Date());
    });
```

This will keep printing an output as follows:

```
2016-11-23T21:21:43.291Z
2016-11-23T21:21:44.315Z
2016-11-23T21:21:45.319Z
```

It works fine and solves our problem, but remember the problem–We wanted an observable to generate and print the current date to the console. Unfortunately, bacon.js doesn't have any observable that could generate the current date every given second, but we can use an operator to change the empty object to the current date. The return of this operator will be a new observable that will emit the current date every second, which is exactly what we wanted from the beginning. Then, we can use the onValue() method to subscribe to this operator in order to print the current date.

Luckily, such an operator exists and it is one of the most commonly used operators as well. It's called the map() operator. It lets you add a function to map an event emitted in another object. It has the following signature:

```
eventStream.map(handler);
```

The handler in the signature is a function that receives the emitted event and returns a new object to substitute the original event (so basically, we **map** an input to an output). You can see this illustrated in the following diagram:

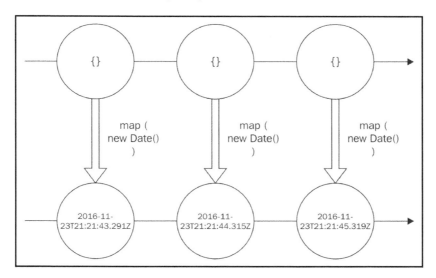

This diagram describes exactly how we want our observable to work. We use the Bacon.inverval() method to generate a new observable that will emit the current date using the map() function. This function is executed every time an object is emitted.

Looking at this diagram makes it a lot easier to understand how we can use the `map()` function to implement the desired behavior. We will need to do some minor changes in our original code to create a new EventStream using the `map()` operator, and change our subscription to only log the emitted event. So, the final implementation of the described diagram using the `map()` operator is as follows:

```
Bacon
    .interval(1000)
    .map(
    (i)=> new Date()
)
    .onValue((date)=>console.log(date));
```

This gives you the same kind of output as from the previous code:

```
2016-11-23T21:21:43.291Z
2016-11-23T21:21:44.315Z
2016-11-23T21:21:45.319Z
```

In this section, I want to show you an example of reusing an `eventStream`. To do this, we will slightly change our original problem. Now, we want to print only those dates where the seconds are even. To do this, we will need a new operator: the `filter()` operator. This operator lets you create a new observable by omitting some events that you are not interested in. It has the following signature:

```
eventStream.filter(handler);
```

Here, `handler` is a function that receives the emitted event as an input and returns `true` or `false` (actually, any truthy or falsy value). So, because we want to print only the dates where the seconds are even, we will pass the following handler as an argument to the `filter` operator:

```
(date)=>date.getSeconds() % 2 == 0
```

As you can see, this function receives the current date as an argument and gets the seconds part of this date. Also, it uses the `mod` operator to decide whether it is an even number or not.

 Notice that one of the advantages of this approach is the creation of small functions to implement each part of our code. This makes our code more testable, as we can easily create unit tests for each of these functions.

Now, to implement this new observable that emits only even dates, all we need to do is chain the `filter()` function to our previous observable in order to create a new observable that we can subscribe to finally print what we want. You can see the use of this `filter()` operator in the following diagram:

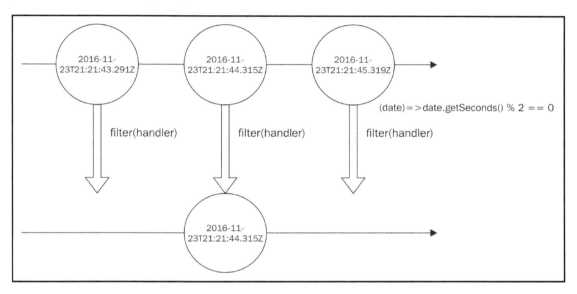

As you can see in this diagram, on the created observable, we don't emit the dates where the seconds are odd numbers. For this reason, we don't have their circles. Now, let's change our code using the `map()` function to use the `filter()` operator as well. This can be easily done with the following code:

```
Bacon
    .interval(1000)
    .map(
    (i)=> new Date()
)
.filter(
    (date)=>date.getSeconds() % 2 == 0
)
.onValue((date)=>console.log(date));
```

If you run this code in a node program, you will see a result like this:

```
2016-11-23T22:08:56.677Z
2016-11-23T22:08:58.715Z
2016-11-23T22:09:00.723Z
```

 Notice that our new output contains only dates with even seconds.

This output is a little confusing. It might be hard to see that it prints only dates with even seconds (because the last part is milliseconds and not seconds). So, let's make a last change in our code. As you might expect, we can use the same operator we used before. To show this, let's use the `map()` operator again to generate a string from the date. Now we want to change our output to something like this:

```
The number in the second part of the date XXX is YYY which is as
even number
```

To do this, let's chain our filtered observable with a `map()` operator to generate this string for each event in the observable. The new observable can be represented by the following diagram:

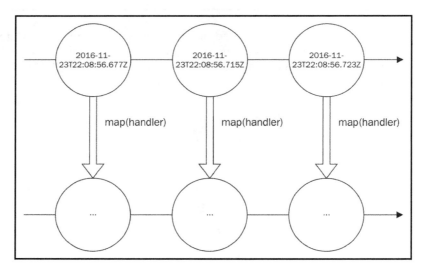

The `handler` function will be used to generate the final string from the date. As the result string is big, I decided to omit it in the result circle, but it will follow the pattern I've described. So, first our `handler` function on the `map()` function should be as follows:

```
(date)=> 'The number in the second part of the date ' +
    date.toISOString() + ' is ' + date.getSeconds() +
' which is as even number'
```

Now, all we have to do is change our last observable with the `map()` operator. We can do this as follows:

```
Bacon
    .interval(1000)
    .map(
    (i)=> new Date()
)
.filter(
    (date)=>date.getSeconds() % 2 == 0
)
.map(
    (date)=> 'The number in the second part of the date ' +
    date.toISOString() + ' is ' + date.getSeconds() +
' which is as even number'
)
.onValue((date)=>console.log(date));
```

Running this code will display the following output, which accentuates the seconds part, making it easier for us to see that it really is an even number:

```
The number in the second part of the date 2016-11-23T22:29:42.694Z
        is 42 which is as even number
The number in the second part of the date 2016-11-23T22:29:44.749Z
        is 44 which is as even number
The number in the second part of the date 2016-11-23T22:29:46.757Z
        is 46 which is as even number
```

The bacon.js has a lot of built-in operators. You can see their descriptions in their APIs. In this section, we only wanted to show how you can use operators to create new observables. We will see a few more operators in depth in the chapters which follows, using RxJS.

Reusing observables

In the previous section, we saw how we can use operators to create new observables, but until this moment, we have never tried reusing an observable. To do this, I propose a change in the program we created in the previous section. We still want to print the string for every date where the seconds part is an even number. But now, let's also print the string `a second has passed` every second. To do this, we can use another `Bacon.interval` call to generate a new observable that emits an empty object every second. Once this is done, we can map each object in the observable to the string we want and finally subscribe to print, as you can see in the following code:

```
Bacon
    .interval(1000)
    .map(
    ()=> 'a second has passed'
)
.onValue((str)=> console.log(str));
```

If you add the preceding code to the last program, you will see the following output:

```
a second has passed
The number in the second part of the date 2016-11-23T22:42:18.683Z
    is 18 which is as even number
a second has passed
a second has passed
The number in the second part of the date 2016-11-23T22:42:20.696Z
    is 20 which is as even number
a second has passed
a second has passed
The number in the second part of the date 2016-11-23T22:42:22.702Z
    is 22 which is as even number
```

This solution is okay, but we can reuse the first `Bacon.interval()`, storing it in a variable. This way, we don't have to keep repeating this code every time we want a source of events emitting every second, using a variable as follows:

```
var emitsEverySecondStream = Bacon.interval(1000);
```

We can create better code by reusing this variable as follows:

```
var emitsEverySecondStream = Bacon.interval(1000);
emitsEverySecondStream.map(
    (i)=> new Date()
)
.filter(
    (date)=>date.getSeconds() % 2 == 0
)
```

```
.map(
    (date)=> 'The number in the second part of the date ' +
    date.toISOString() + ' is ' + date.getSeconds() +
' which is as even number'
)
.onValue((date)=>console.log(date));
emitsEverySecondStream.map(
    ()=> 'a second has passed'
)
.onValue((str)=> console.log(str));
```

This code gives us the same kind of output as from the previous example.

Another important feature when reusing observables is the ability to add multiple subscribers to the same observable. You can see this happening in the following code:

```
var eventStream = Bacon
        .interval(1000)
        .map(
        ()=> 'a second has passed'
    );
eventStream
    .onValue((str)=>console.log('Subscriber 1 prints => ' + str));
eventStream
    .onValue((str)=>console.log('Subscriber 2 prints => ' + str));
eventStream
    .onValue((str)=>console.log('Subscriber 3 prints => ' + str));
```

In this code, we added three subscriptions to the same EventStream. This will give us the following output:

```
Subscriber 1 prints => a second has passed
Subscriber 2 prints => a second has passed
Subscriber 3 prints => a second has passed
Subscriber 1 prints => a second has passed
Subscriber 2 prints => a second has passed
Subscriber 3 prints => a second has passed
```

 Remember that the onValue() function returns a function to unsubscribe that function from the observable. So if you want, you can unsubscribe from each subscription individually without affecting other subscriptions.

Observables' lazy evaluation

In bacon.js, an observable doesn't emit any event unless someone is subscribed to listen to it. We can easily check this behavior using `doAction()`. This operator lets us run an arbitrary function every time an event is emitted from an observable.

If you create an observable from an array and add a `doAction()` operator to log your events then, without a subscription, it will print nothing to the console. So if you run the following code, you will see your program doesn't give you any output:

```
Bacon
    .fromArray([1,2,3])
    .doAction((value)=>
        console.log('running doAction')
    );
```

As you can see in this code, we have no subscriber for the EventStream. This is why no event is emitted. However, if we add a subscriber to this EventStream, we will see the program print `running doAction` for each value:

```
Bacon
    .fromArray([1,2,3])
    .doAction((value)=>
        console.log('running doAction')
    )
    .log();
```

The preceding code gives you the following output:

```
running doAction
1
running doAction
2
running doAction
3
<end>
```

 It is really important to keep this behavior in mind because ignoring this can lead to bugs that are really hard to identify.

Summary

In this chapter, you learned the basics of functional reactive programming using the `bacon.js` library. We wanted to give you the taste of functional reactive programming and also get your hands dirty with a lot of different examples.

You learned about observables and the different types of observables that bacon.js has implemented. You also learned about some of the built-in methods that help you create observables in bacon.js and also how you can create your own observable using the `fromBinder()` method.

Apart from this, you also learned how to subscribe and unsubscribe from an observable, how to use operators to transform an observable, and the importance of reuse in this context.

In the next chapter, we will start using RxJS as it gives us more tools for functional reactive programming. We will see how it compares with bacon.js and understand the basics of this new tool.

3
A World Full of Changes - Reactive Extensions to the Rescue

In the previous chapter, you learned the very basics of functional reactive programming, using the `bacon.js` library. We discussed what is an observable and saw two different flavors of it in the `bacon.js` library (EventStream and Property). We also looked at how to create observables from common event sources (interval, array, or user input) and even from any other possible source (using the `fromBinder()` method).

After an introduction to observables, we looked at how to subscribe to it. You can react to events, errors, or even detect the end of an observable when you subscribe to it. So, you learned how to create an observer for your observables.

One of the really important lessons from the previous chapter was the usage of diagrams to explain how observables and operators occur, along with text explanations and example code. Understanding diagrams is the key to understanding the behavior of operators and observables; you will see a lot of diagrams throughout the book. Read this section with special attention. Read it again in case you're not comfortable with it yet, but don't be afraid if it seems complicated (it seemed that way to me the first time I saw it). You will keep seeing it with text explanations and will eventually learn how it works.

The previous chapter added a lot of new concepts to your toolbox, and one of these was operators. The usage of operators to transform your events into something completely new gives you the taste of functional reactive programming and lets you see how powerful and composable it is. If you liked the initial operators you used, then be happy; we will see a lot more operators in the upcoming chapters. Operators are the backbone of functional reactive programming and they help you write cleaner, concise, and testable code with ease.

Finally, we saw the laziness of observables in the `bacon.js` library. We will talk about the behavior of observables in RxJS in this chapter, so don't worry.

This chapter will introduce you to the world of Reactive Extensions. In this book, we will base our implementation on RxJS. However, Reactive Extensions is an agnostic framework (this means it has implementations for several languages), so a lot of the concepts described here can be used in other platforms (such as RxJava, RxSwift, and so on). This makes learning Reactive Extensions (and functional reactive programming) really useful, as you can use it to improve your code in different platforms.

The focus in this chapter is to teach you the different types of observables possible in the RxJS world. You will see that they differ a little bit from the observables of bacon.js but are easy to use. You will also learn how to react to events in our observables using observers and how to finish your observers.

This chapter will cover the following points:

- The different types of observables in the context of Reactive Extensions and the difference between them
- Using the RxJS API to create observables
- Reacting to events in our observables
- Reacting to errors in our observables

RxJS observables

RxJS lets you have even more control over the source of your data. In this section, we will learn the differences between RxJS Observables and bacon.js EventStreams and Properties. We will also learn some different flavors of Observables and how we can better control their life cycle.

Difference between bacon.js and RxJS observables

In `Chapter 2`, *Reacting for the First Time,* you learned that an observable is basically an abstraction over possible asynchronous data. The observable gives you the power to transform data using different operators and take an action when a piece of new data becomes available, using a subscriber. The `bacon.js` library uses the term **subscriber** to the object listening to incoming data, but on Reactive Extensions, we will use a different term; we will call it Observer.

Conceptually, there is no difference between the two. Basically, it was just names chosen by the developers of both libraries; however, it is important that you're aware of both the names as you will see both being used in the documentation of the libraries.

In bacon.js, we saw two different flavors of observables:

- EventStreams
- Properties

In RxJS, we will always talk about:

- Observables
- Observers

 In this chapter, you will also learn more about three special objects in RxJS. They are called **Subject**, **Disposable**, and **Scheduler**.

Hot and cold observables

In bacon.js, an observable only emits a value when a subscriber subscribes to it; therefore, we will call it a **cold observables**. In Reactive Extensions, things can become a little trickier: we have both hot and cold observables.

A hot observable is an observable that propagates the data independently, irrespective of whether we have some Observer attached to it or not. An example of a hot observable is an observable created from mouse movements.

A cold observable, on the other hand, is an observable that fires the same sequence for all the subscribers. An example of a cold observable is an observable created from an array.

This behavior is important to understand, and RxJS has special methods to replay events in a hot observable or turn a cold observable into a hot observable.

Installing RxJS

RxJS is divided into modules. This way, you can create your own bundle with only the modules you're interested in. In this book, we will always use the official bundle with all the contents from RxJS; by doing so, we'll not have to worry about whether a certain module exists in our bundle or not. So, let's follow the steps described here to install RxJS.

To install it on your server, just run the following command inside a node project:

```
npm i rx@4.1.0 -save
```

To add it to a HTML page, just paste the following code snippet inside your HTML:

```
<script src="https://cdnjs.cloudflare.com/ajax/libs/rxjs/4.1.0/rx.all.js">
</script>
```

 For those using other package managers, you can install RxJS from Bower or NuGet.

If you're running inside a node program, you need to have the RxJS library in each JavaScript file that you want to use. To do this, add the following line to the beginning of your JavaScript file:

```
var Rx = require('rx');
```

The preceding line will be omitted in all examples, as we expect you to have added it before testing the sample code.

Creating an observable

Here we will see a list of methods to create an observable from common event sources. This is not an exhaustive list, but it contains the most important ones.

You can see all the available methods on the RxJS GitHub page (`https://github.com/Reactive-Extensions/RxJS`).

Creating an observable from iterable objects

We can create an observable from iterable objects using the `from()` method. An iterable in JavaScript can be an array (or an array-like object) or other iterates added in ES6 (such as `Set()` and `map()`). The `from()` method has the following signature:

```
Rx.Observable.from(iterable, [mapFunction], [context], [scheduler]);
```

Usually, you will pass only the first argument. Others arguments are optional; you can see them here:

- `iterable`: This is the `iterable` object to be converted into an observable (can be an array, set, map, and so on)
- `mapFunction`: This is a function to be called for every element in the array to map it to a different value
- `context`: This object is to be used when `mapFunction` is provided
- `scheduler`: This is used to iterate the input sequence

Don't worry if you don't know what a scheduler is. We will see how it changes our observables, but we will discuss it later in this chapter. For now, focus only on the other arguments of this function.

Now let's see some examples on how we can create observables from iterables.

To create an observable from an array, you can use the following code:

```
Rx.Observable
    .from([0,1,2])
    .subscribe((a)=>console.log(a));
```

This code prints the following output:

```
0
1
2
```

Now let's introduce a minor change in our code, to add the `mapFunction` argument to it, instead of creating an observable to propagate the elements of this array. Let's use `mapFunction` to propagate the double of each element of the following array:

```
Rx.Observable
    .from([0,1,2], (a) => a*2)
    .subscribe((a)=>console.log(a));
```

This prints the following output:

```
0
2
4
```

We can also use this method to create an observable from an `arguments` object. To do this, we need to run `from()` in a function. This way, we can access the `arguments` object of the function. We can implement it with the following code:

```
var observableFromArgumentsFactory = function(){
    return Rx.Observable.from(arguments);
};
observableFromArgumentsFactory(0,1,2)
    .subscribe((a)=>console.log(a));
```

If we run this code, we will see the following output:

```
0
1
2
```

One last usage of this method is to create an observable from either `Set()` or `Map()`. These data structures were added to ES6. We can implement it for a `set` as follows:

```
var set = new Set([0,1,2]);
Rx.Observable
    .from(set)
    .subscribe((a)=>console.log(a));
```

This code prints the following output:

```
0
1
2
```

We can also use a `map` as an argument for the `from()` method, as follows:

```
var map = new Map([['key0',0],['key1',1],['key2',2]]);
Rx.Observable
    .from(map)
    .subscribe((a)=>console.log(a));
```

This prints all the key-value tuples on this `map`:

```
[ 'key0', 0 ]
[ 'key1', 1 ]
[ 'key2', 2 ]
```

All observables created from this method are cold observables. As discussed before, this means it fires the same sequence for all the observers. To test this behavior, create an `observable` and add an Observer to it; add another observer to it after a second:

```
var observable = Rx.Observable.from([0,1,2]);

observable.subscribe((a)=>console.log('first subscriber receives => '+a));

setTimeout(()=>{
    observable.subscribe((a)=>console.log('second subscriber receives => '+a));
},1000);
```

If you run this code, you will see the following output in your console, showing both the subscribers receiving the same data as expected:

```
first subscriber receives => 0
first subscriber receives => 1
first subscriber receives => 2
second subscriber receives => 0
second subscriber receives => 1
second subscriber receives => 2
```

Creating an observable from a sequence factory

Now that we have discussed how to create an observable from a sequence, let's see how we can create an observable from a sequence factory. RxJS has a built-in method called `generate()` that lets you create an observable from an iteration (such as a `for()` loop). This method has the following signature:

```
Rx.Observable.generate(initialState, conditionFunction, iterationFunction,
resultFactory, [scheduler]);
```

In this method, the only optional parameter is the last one. A brief description of all the parameters is as follows:

- `initialState`: This can be any object, it is the first object used in the iteration
- `conditionFunction`: This is a function with the condition to stop the iteration
- `iterationFunction`: This is a function to be used on each element to iterate
- `resultFactory`: This is a function whose return is passed to the sequence
- `scheduler`: This is an optional scheduler

Before checking out an example code for this method, let's see some code that implements one of the most basic constructs in a program: a `for()` loop. This is used to generate an array from an initial value to a final value. We can produce this array with the following code:

```
var resultArray=[];
for(var i=0;i < 3;i++){
    resultArray.push(i)
}
console.log(resultArray);
```

This code prints the following output:

```
[0,1,2]
```

When you create a `for()` loop, you basically give to it the following: an initial state (the first argument), the condition to stop the iteration (the second argument), how to iterate over the value (the third argument), and what to do with the value (block). Its usage is very similar to the `generate()` method. Let's do the same thing, but using the `generate()` method and creating an observable instead of an array:

```
Rx.Observable.generate(
    0,
    (i) => i<3,
    (i) => i+1,
    (i) => i
).subscribe((i) => console.log(i));
```

This code will print the following output:

```
0
1
2
```

Creating an observable using range ()

Another common source of data for observables are ranges. With the `range()` method, we can easily create an observable for a sequence of values in a range. The `range()` method has the following signature:

```
Rx.Observable.range(first, count, [scheduler]);
```

The last parameter in the following list is the only optional parameter in this method:

- `first`: This is the initial integer value in the sequence
- `count`: This is the number of sequential integers to be iterated from the beginning of the sequence
- `scheduler`: This is used to generate the values

We can create an observable using a range with the following code:

```
Rx.Observable
    .range(0, 4)
    .subscribe((i)=>console.log(i));
```

This prints the following output:

```
0
1
2
3
```

Creating an observable using period of time

In the previous chapter, we discussed how to create timed sequences in bacon.js. In RxJS, we have two different methods to implement observables emitting values with a given interval. The first method is `interval()`. This method emits an infinite sequence of integers starting from one every *x* milliseconds; it has the following signature:

```
Rx.Observable.interval(interval, [scheduler]);
```

The interval parameter is mandatory, and the second argument is optional:

- `interval`: This is an integer number to be used as the interval between the values of this sequence
- `scheduler`: This is used to generate the values

Run the following code:

```
Rx.Observable
    .interval(1000)
    .subscribe((i)=> console.log(i));
```

You will see an output as follows; you will have to stop your program (hitting Ctrl+C) or it will keep sending events:

```
0
1
2
```

The `interval()` method sends the first value of the sequence after the given period of interval and keeps sending values after each interval.

RxJS also has a method called `timer()`. This method lets you specify a due time to start the sequence or even generate an observable of only one value emitted after the due time has elapsed. It has the following signature:

```
Rx.Observable.timer(dueTime, [interval], [scheduler]);
```

Here are the parameters:

- `dueTime`: This can be a date object or an integer. If it is a date object, then it means it is the absolute time to start the sequence; if it is an integer, then it specifies the number of milliseconds to wait for before you could send the first element of the sequence.
- `interval`: This is an integer denoting the time between the elements. If it is not specified, it generates only one event.
- `scheduler`: This is used to produce the values.

We can create an observable from the `timer()` method with the following code:

```
Rx.Observable
    .timer(1000,500)
    .subscribe((i)=> console.log(i));
```

You will see an output that will be similar to the following; you will have to stop your program or it will keep sending events:

```
0
1
2
```

We can also use this method to generate only one value and finish the sequence. We can do this omitting the `interval` parameter, as shown in the following code:

```
Rx.Observable
    .timer(1000)
    .subscribe((i)=> console.log(i));
```

If you run this code, it will only print 0 in your console and finish.

Creating an observable from callbacks

In JavaScript, we have a lot of APIs that use callbacks to let you control the flow of the application. We can use functional reactive programming to have better control of it. We can use observables to wrap callbacks (following the Node.js callback pattern). This way, we can reuse and compose these callbacks.

To do so, we can use the `fromCallback()` method. It has the following signature:

```
Rx.Observable.fromCallback(func,[context],[selector]);
```

The first argument is mandatory and the next two are optional. They are as follows:

- `func`: This is the function that usually receives a callback when it finishes
- `context`: This is the context to be used in the callback
- `selector`: This is a function that takes the arguments from the callback to produce a single item to be propagated by this observable

Before showing examples of the usage of this method, let's create our own function accepting a `callback` function, as follows:

```
var myAsyncComputation = function(name,callback){
    setTimeout(()=>{
        callback(null,'Finished computation for '+name);
    },100);
};
```

The `myAsyncComputation` variable holds a function that accepts a `callback` function. It calls this `callback` function after 100 milliseconds with a success message: `Finished computation for SOME_NAME`. To test our function, we can just call it in the following way:

```
myAsyncComputation('John Doe',(err,result)=>console.log(result));
```

This will print the `Finished computation for John Doe` message.

 Remember, callbacks can receive two parameters: the first is `error` (if any error has occurred) and the second is `result`, representing the result of the asynchronous computation made by the function.

Now let's create an observable for our asynchronous function, as follows:

```
var observableFromCallback =
Rx.Observable.fromCallback(myAsyncComputation);

observableFromCallback('John Doe')
        .subscribe((result)=> console.log(result));
```

If you run this code, you will see the following message printed on the console:

```
[ null, 'Finished computation for John Doe' ]
```

This happens because as we discussed, a callback receives two arguments: the first is the error (if any) and the second is the successful result. If we don't want to propagate both the values, we can use the selector parameter from the `fromCallback()` method to map the response in a different way:

```
var observableFromCallback = Rx.Observable.
        fromCallback(myAsyncComputation, null, (error,result)=>result);
observableFromCallback('John Doe')
        .subscribe((result)=> console.log(result));
```

Now we added an argument to omit the error, so when we run this code, we will see the following output:

```
Finished computation for John Doe
```

Creating an observable from a promise

The promises are objects that hold the result of an asynchronous computation. They are becoming more common now. One of the cool things about promises is that you can compose them with other promises or synchronous values, giving you an extra layer of abstraction over asynchronous computations. We can wrap a promise into an observable. This provides us a lot more power to handle the result of our computation using the operators from RxJS.

To do this, we can use the `fromPromise()` built-in method. This method can turn any A+ Promise into an observable.

 Promises/A+ is a specification of promises. All the famous promises libraries in JavaScript follow this pattern; it is the same pattern followed by the standard ES6 promise.

This method has the following signature:

```
Rx.Observable.fromPromise(promise);
```

It receives only one parameter:

- `promise`: This is a Promises/A+ object or a factory function that returns an A+ Promise object.

To create an observable from a promise, use the following code:

```
Rx.Observable
    .fromPromise(Promise.resolve('Hello World'))
    .subscribe((result)=> console.log(result));
```

This prints the following output:

Hello World

We can also use this method to create an observable from a factory function returning a promise, as you can see in the following code:

```
var promiseFactory = () => Promise.resolve('Hello World')
Rx.Observable
    .fromPromise(promiseFactory)
    .subscribe((result)=> console.log(result));
```

When you run this code, you will see the following output:

Hello World

Creating empty observables

Sometimes, when composing multiple observables, you might need to create an empty observable. You can do this in RxJS using two different methods. The first one is the `empty()` method; this method will only fire an `onComplete` event.

The following code creates an observable that finishes and doesn't propagate any value:

```
Rx.Observable.empty();
```

Sometimes you might need an observable that wouldn't emit any value and would never terminate. To create this kind of observable, you can use the `never()` method:

```
Rx.Observable.never();
```

 These two methods are used more for composition or as a fallback to prevent the absence of an observable. The only difference between the two is that only the first one terminates.

Creating an observable from a single value

When composing multiple observables or mocking observables for testing purposes, you might need to create an observable that would emit only one value and then terminate itself. RxJS has two methods to implement this behavior: the `return()` method and the `just()` method. They work exactly in the same way and have the following signature:

```
Rx.Observable.return(value, [scheduler]);
Rx.Observable.just(value, [scheduler]);
```

The first argument is mandatory and the second is optional:

- `value`: This can be any object; it is the value to be emitted on the sequence
- `scheduler`: This is used to emit the value

The following code illustrates an example of this method:

```
Rx.Observable
    .just('Hello World')
    .subscribe((i)=> console.log(i));
```

This code uses the `just()` method, but we can also use the `return()` method with a simple change in it:

```
Rx.Observable
    .return('Hello World')
    .subscribe((i)=> console.log(i));
```

If you run any of these code lines, you will see the `Hello World` message printed in your console.

Creating an observable from a factory function

There is a method in RxJS where you can create an observable from a function that returns an observable or an observable factory function; it is called `defer()`. The signature of this method is as follows:

```
Rx.Observable.defer(factoryFunction);
```

It receives only one parameter, and this parameter is mandatory:

- `factoryFunction`: This is a function that returns an observable

The following code shows an implementation of this method:

```
Rx.Observable
    .defer(function(){
        return Rx.Observable.just('Hello World');
    })
    .subscribe((data)=>console.log(data));
```

If you run this code, you will see the following output:

Hello World

As the name implies, the `defer()` method only calls the factory function when an Observer subscribes to it.

Creating an observable from arbitrary arguments

You have already learned how to create an observable from a sequence using the `from()` method, but there is a way to create an observable from an arbitrary sequence of arguments. We can do this using the `of()` method.

This method creates an observable that emits each argument passed to it.

The `of()` method has the following signature:

```
Rx.Observable.of(...args);
```

The three dots before `args` illustrate an arbitrary number of arguments.

- `...args`: This refers to any number of objects

The following code shows an implementation of the `of()` method:

```
Rx.Observable
    .of(0,1,2)
    .subscribe((i)=>console.log(i));
```

If you run this code, you will see the following output:

```
0
1
2
```

Now let's see what happens if we use the `of()` method with only one parameter on it.

Say you run the following code:

```
Rx.Observable
    .of('Hello World')
    .subscribe((i)=>console.log(i));
```

When you do this, you will see the following output:

```
Hello World
```

As you can see, if you run the `of()` method with only one argument, it works the same way as the `just()` method.

Now you might be wondering what happens if you run the `of()` method without any argument. To check this, let's run the following code:

```
Rx.Observable
    .of()
    .subscribe((i)=>console.log(i));
```

If you run the preceding code, your program will finish without any output in the console. So if you run the `of()` method without any argument, it will have the same behavior as the `empty()` method.

Remember that the `empty()` method creates an observable without any element and ends it, while the `never()` method creates an empty observable that never ends. So creating an observable using the `of()` method without any argument is the same as creating an observable using the `empty()` method.

Creating an observable from an error

We can use an observable to wrap an error; this way, we will have all the operators and compositions of the concerned observable.

RxJS gives us two methods to wrap an error. Both work in exactly the same way and are basically aliases of each other.

The methods to wrap an error to an observable are `throw()` and `throwError()`. We also have a method called `throwException()`, but this method is deprecated and should not be used anymore.

Both methods have the same signature, as follows:

```
Rx.Observable.throw(err, [scheduler]);
Rx.Observable.throwError(err, [scheduler]);
```

The first method is the error you want to wrap around the observable and it is mandatory; the second is optional:

- `err`: This is any object representing an error
- `scheduler`: This is used to generate the sequence of the observable

Lets see a code snippet that uses the `throw()` method:

```
Rx.Observable
    .throw(new Error('AN ERROR HAPPENED'))
    .subscribe((data)=>console.log(data));
```

If you run the preceding code, you will see an error stack trace on your console and your program will finish.

Now let's introduce a minor change in our code.

The `subscribe()` method from RxJS can receive a second function to react to errors, so let's add another function to print the message of the error:

```
Rx.Observable
    .throw(new Error('AN ERROR HAPPENED'))
    .subscribe(
    (data)=>console.log(data),
    (err)=>{
        console.log('Running the subscription function for error');
        console.log(err.message)
    }
);
```

If you run the code, you will see the following error message in your console:

```
Running the subscription function for error
AN ERROR HAPPENED
```

 Later in this chapter, we'll see the possible parameter for the `subscribe()` method.

In our example, we passed an `Error` object for the `throw()` method, but what happens when we pass another type of object, such as a number? To answer this question, let's introduce a minor change in our code:

```
Rx.Observable
    .throw(1)
    .subscribe(
    (data)=>console.log(data),
    (err)=>{
        console.log('Running the subscription function for error');
        console.log(err.message)
    }
);
```

If you run the preceding code, you will see the following output:

```
Running the subscription function for error
undefined
```

So as you can see, it doesn't matter what is the object. You can use the `throw()` method to wrap any object as an error. Using another object to represent an error is an anti-pattern, so be careful and always wrap your errors inside an `Error` object.

Never throw a string (or any object) without wrapping it in an `Error` object.

Creating observables from DOM events (or EventEmitter)

One of the most important usages of RxJS in frontend applications is to create observables from user input such as mouse clicks, mouse moves, or keystrokes.

RxJS can bind to DOM elements, jQuery (or Zepto.js) elements, Ember elements, or Angular elements, if any of these libraries are present. RxJS will attempt to detect the libraries automatically.

This method can also be used to bind to a Node.js EventEmitter.

The method `fromEvent()` is used to create observables from DOM elements. This method has the following signature:

```
Rx.Observable.fromEvent(element,eventName,[mapFunction]);
```

The first two parameters are mandatory, and the last one is optional:

- `element`: This represents either the DOM element, jQuery element, Angular element, Ember element, NodeList, or EventEmitter to attach the event
- `eventName`: This is a string representing the event
- `mapFunction`: This is a function that takes arguments from EventEmitter and maps it to a single value

To use the `fromEvent()` method, create an HTML page with a single element, as follows:

```
<html>
    <head></head>
    <body>
        <div id="myDiv">Foo</div>
        <script
src="https://cdnjs.cloudflare.com/ajax/libs/rxjs/4.1.0/rx.all.js"></script>
    </body>
</html>
```

Now let's show an alert every time the user clicks on the word **Foo**. In the first example, let's create an observable from a DOM element.

Add a script tag to your HTML file to listen to the click on <div>:

```
Rx.Observable
    .fromEvent(document.getElementById('myDiv'),'click')
    .subscribe(function(e){
        alert('Clicked');
    });
```

Open this file in your browser and click on the word **Foo**; once you click on it, an alert will pop up on your screen.

 Remember, before adding this code to your HTML file, you have to add RxJS as a script to your page.

Now let's use a jQuery element instead of a DOM element. Change your <script> tag to use the following code:

```
Rx.Observable
    .fromEvent($('#myDiv'),'click')
    .subscribe(function(e){
        alert('Clicked');
    });
```

Open this HTML file in your browser and click on the word **Foo**; once you click on it, an alert will pop up on your screen.

 Remember, before adding this code to your HTML file, you have to add jQuery as a script to your page.

As you can see, you don't need any changes to make RxJS support the jQuery element; it just works out of the box.

We can also use the `fromEvent()` method on Node.js EventEmitters. To illustrate this usage, let's read a file and print its content to the console using RxJS:

```
var fs = require('fs');
var Rx = require('rx');
var readStream = fs.createReadStream(__filename,'utf8');
Rx.Observable
    .fromEvent(readStream, 'data')
    .subscribe((i)=> console.log(i));
```

In this example, we first imported the `fs` module to read files and the RxJS module. Then, we created `readStream` from our own file (the `__filename` variable holds the location of the current file) and we added the string `utf8` to read our file as a string (if we omit this, it will read the file as bytes). And finally, we used the `fromEvent()` method to create an observable from this stream, listening to all the events of the type `data`. We need to subscribe to the observable in order to print the content in the console.

If you run the preceding code, you will see your own program printed in the console.

Now lets make a minor change in our code. If we remove the `utf8` string in the `createReadStream()` method and re-execute the program, we will see an output as follows:

```
<Buffer 76 61 72 20 66 73 20 3d 20 72 65 71 75 69 72 65 28 27 66 73
27 29 3b 0a 76 61 72 20 52 78 20 3d 20 72 65 71 75 69 72 65 28 27
72 78 27 29 3b 0a 0a 76 ... >
```

We already know we can add the `utf8` string as a parameter to make the `createReadStream()` method convert it into a string.

If we haven't, we could use RxJS.

In JavaScript, the buffer object has a method called `toString()` to convert it into a string using the given character encoding. So if I want to convert a buffer into an `utf8` string, all I have to do is write it as follows:

```
var myString = myBuffer.toString('utf8');
```

The `fromEvent()` method can receive a third parameter to map the input from the EventEmitter to another value before propagating it to the listeners.

We can use this method to avoid marking readStream as an utf8 string, and we can do this only in the observable. To do this, use the following code:

```
var fs = require('fs');
var Rx = require('rx');

var readStream = fs.createReadStream(__filename);
Rx.Observable
    .fromEvent(readStream, 'data', (chunk)=>chunk.toString('utf8'))
    .subscribe((i)=> console.log(i));
```

Creating an observable from an arbitrary source

In the previous chapter, we discussed how to implement an observable from an arbitrary source in bacon.js, using the fromBinder event. On RxJS, we can also create an observable from any source that we want using the create() method. There is also an alias for this method, called createWithDisposable.

The create() method has the following signature:

```
Rx.Observable.create(sourceFunction);
```

This method accepts only one parameter and it is mandatory:

- sourceFunction: This is a function that receives an object capable of pushing data into an observable

We can create an observable with the create() method using the following code:

```
Rx.Observable.create(function(source){
    source.onNext(0);
    source.onNext(1);
    source.onNext(2);
    source.onCompleted();
}).subscribe((i)=> console.log(i));
```

If you run this code, you will see the following output:

```
0
1
2
```

We can also use it to send errors to the observable, as you can see in this code:

```
Rx.Observable.create(function(source){
    source.onNext(0);
    source.onNext(1);
    source.onError(new Error('ops'));
    source.onNext(2);
    source.onCompleted();
}).subscribe(
    (i)=> console.log(i),
    (err)=> console.log('An error happened: '+err.message )
);
```

If you run this code, you will see the following output:

```
0
1
An error happened: ops
```

 As you can see, the observable stops sending data in case there are errors. In later chapters, we will see how we can recover from errors.

Sometimes when creating an observable, you might need to release some allocated resources (such as database connections or file handlers). To do this, RxJS has a special type of object called Disposable.

The `create()` method lets you define a function (or a Disposable object) to be fired when you no longer want to hold the resources you just allocated.

To do this, all you have to do is return a function (or a Disposable object) and call the `dispose()` method of the subscription, as seen in the following code:

```
var observable = Rx.Observable.create(function(source){
    source.onNext(0);
    source.onNext(1);
    source.onNext(2);
    source.onCompleted();
    return function(){
        console.log('dispose called: releasing connections or other
```

```
resources');
    };
});
var subscription = observable.subscribe(
        (i)=> console.log(i)
);
subscription.dispose();
```

If you run this code, you will see the following output:

```
0
1
2
dispose called: releasing connections or other resources
```

As can be seen, the function returned by the parameter passed to the `create()` method is called when you call the `dispose()` method on the subscription of the observable. We could also return a Disposable object instead of a function to be executed when the `dispose()` method of the subscription is called.

We will learn more about Disposable objects later in this chapter.

Subscribing to changes (Observer)

To listen to data on an observable, we must call the `subscribe()` method. This method returns a subscription, which we can use later to stop reacting to the incoming data if we are no longer interested in it.

The `subscribe()` method of observables has the following signature:

```
observable.subscribe(onNext,onError,onCompleted);
```

All parameters are optional and can be omitted if we are not interested in this type of event:

- `onNext`: This is a function to be called every time new data is propagated through the observable
- `onError`: This is a function to be called every time an error occurs in the observable
- `onCompleted`: This is a function to be called when the observable is completed

The easiest way to subscribe to an observable is to just pass the `onNext` parameter (as we have been doing in most of our code snippets in this chapter):

```
Rx.Observable
    .just('Hello World!!!')
    .subscribe((message)=>console.log(message));
```

If you run the preceding code, it will print the `Hello World!!!` message in your console.

We can also add an `onError` function to be called when an error happens:

```
Rx.Observable
    .throw(new Error('ops'))
    .subscribe(
        (message)=>console.log(message),
        (err)=>console.log('An error happened: '+err.message)
    );
```

If you run this code, you will see the following output in your console:

An error happened: ops

Lastly, we can also add the `onCompleted()` function to take an action when the observable is completed:

```
Rx.Observable
    .just('Hello World!!!')
    .subscribe(
        (message)=>console.log(message),
        (err)=>console.log('An error happened: '+err.message),
        ()=>console.log('END')
    );
```

If you run this code, you will see the following output:

Hello World!!!
END

All subscriptions have a method called `dispose()`. This method can be used to stop listening to incoming data in the observable. We can test it in the following code:

```
var subscription = Rx.Observable
    .interval(100)
    .subscribe(
        (message)=>console.log(message),
        (err)=>console.log('An error happened: '+err.message),
        ()=>console.log('END')
```

```
        );

    setTimeout(()=>subscription.dispose(),290);
```

As illustrated in the code, we first create an observable that would emit data every 100 milliseconds and we subscribe to it. Then we use the `setTimeout()` function to call the `dispose()` method of this subscription and stop listening to data from the original observable.

If you run this code, you will see the following output in your console:

```
0
1
```

 Remember, the `interval()` method will wait for 100 milliseconds before sending the number 0. Then, it will wait for 100 milliseconds more to send the number 1.

In RxJS, we also have a special class of objects called Observer. Basically, this object wraps the functions `onNext()`, `onError()`, and `onCompleted()` that you use to subscribe to an observable, giving you an extra layer of abstraction.

To create an `observer`, we can use the `create()` method and then use this `observer` to subscribe to an observable, as you can see in following code:

```
var observer = Rx.Observer.create(
        (message)=> console.log(message),
        (err)=>console.log('An error happened: '+err.message),
        ()=>console.log('END')
);

Rx.Observable
    .just('Hello World!!!')
    .subscribe(observer);
```

If you run this code, you will see the following output:

```
Hello World!!!
END
```

 Observer is the object responsible for reacting to data sent by an Observable.

RxJS Subjects

Subjects could be both an Observable and an Observer. They can be seen as a pushable Observable; they let you add more data to be propagated through them.

Subjects expose three important methods: `onNext()`, `onError()`, and `onCompleted()`. These methods can be used to send events through the observable sequence. You can see their usage in the following example:

```
var subject = new Rx.Subject();

subject.subscribe(
    (message)=> console.log(message),
    (err)=>console.log('An error happened: '+err.message),
    ()=>console.log('END')
);

subject.onNext('Hello World!!!');
subject.onCompleted();
```

In this example, we created a new `subject` and subscribed to it, using the `subscribe()` method. Then, we pushed data on this `subject` using the `onNext()` method, and we finally finished it calling the `onCompleted()` method.

If you run this code, you will see the following output:

Hello World!!!
END

We can also propagate an error through a subject using its `onError()` method:

```
var subject = new Rx.Subject();

subject.subscribe(
    (message)=> console.log(message),
    (err)=>console.log('An error happened: '+err.message),
    ()=>console.log('END')
);

subject.onNext('Hello World!!!');
subject.onError(new Error('ops'));
```

First, we propagate the value `Hello World`, which will be printed in the console. Then, we propagate an error. If you run the preceding code, you will see the following output in your console:

```
Hello World!!!
An error happened: ops
```

There is another type of subject called `AsyncSubject()`. It can be used to represent the result of an asynchronous operation. An `AsyncSubject()` can receive only one value, and this value is then cached for all future subscriptions of this subject.

An example of `AsyncSubject()` creation can be seen in the following code:

```
var subject = new Rx.AsyncSubject();

subject.subscribe(
    (message)=> console.log(message),
    (err)=>console.log('An error happened: '+err.message),
    ()=>console.log('END')
);

subject.onNext('Hello World!!!');
subject.onCompleted();
```

As you can see, the only difference to create it–when compared to a Subject–appears on the first line of code, where we use `new Rx.AsyncSubject()` instead of `new Rx.Subject()`. If you run this code, you will see the following output in your console:

```
Hello World!!!
END
```

As discussed earlier, an `AsyncSubject()` must be used to propagate only one piece of data. So let's compare it with a regular Subject.

First, let's see what the output of a Subject would be when we call the `onNext()` method multiple times:

```
var subject = new Rx.Subject();

subject.subscribe(
    (message)=> console.log(message),
    (err)=>console.log('An error happened: '+err.message),
    ()=>console.log('END')
);

subject.onNext(0);
subject.onNext(1);
```

```
subject.onNext(2);
subject.onCompleted();
```

If you run this code, you will have the following content printed in the console:

```
0
1
2
END
```

This shows us that the Observer was fired three times (for elements 0, 1, and 2). Now let's change our code to use an `AsyncSubject()`:

```
var subject = new Rx.AsyncSubject();

subject.subscribe(
    (message)=> console.log(message),
    (err)=>console.log('An error happened: '+err.message),
    ()=>console.log('END')
);

subject.onNext(0);
subject.onNext(1);
subject.onNext(2);
subject.onCompleted();
```

If we look at the console after running this code, we will see the following printed:

```
2
END
```

As expected, an `AsyncSubject()` propagates only one element, and for this reason, it fires the Observer once (with two elements).

Lastly, let's see what happens if we don't call the `onCompleted()` method in our Subjects.

First, let's use a regular subject:

```
var subject = new Rx.Subject();

subject.subscribe(
    (message)=> console.log(message),
    (err)=>console.log('An error happened: '+err.message),
    ()=>console.log('END')
);
```

```
subject.onNext(0);
subject.onNext(1);
subject.onNext(2);
```

If we run this code, we will see the following output:

```
0
1
2
```

We can see that a Subject doesn't wait for the `onCompleted()` method to be called to propagate the elements.

Now let's check out the output of `AsyncSubject()`:

```
var subject = new Rx.AsyncSubject();

subject.subscribe(
    (message)=> console.log(message),
    (err)=>console.log('An error happened: '+err.message),
    ()=>console.log('END')
);

subject.onNext(0);
subject.onNext(1);
subject.onNext(2);
```

If we run this code, nothing is printed in the console, so an `AsyncSubject()` will wait for the `onCompleted()` method before it can start propagating the element. So it's easy to see that when dealing with `AsyncSubject()`, we must always call the `onNext()` and `onCompleted()` methods together.

The easiest way to understand a Subject is to see it as a pushable observable.

RxJS Disposable

The `Disposable` class gives us a method to release allocated resources (database connections, file handlers, and so on). We can do this by calling the `dispose()` method of this object.

In this section, we will use the `dispose()` method to unsubscribe from an observable.

To create a `Disposable`, we can use the `create()` function from `Rx.Disposable`:

```
var disposable = Rx.Disposable
        .create(()=>console.log('Releasing allocated resources'));

disposable.dispose();
```

If you run this code, it will print the following message in your console:

Releasing allocated resources

As discussed earlier in this chapter, we can call the `dispose()` method to unsubscribe from an observable. In some cases, we can even define a `Disposable` to be used when someone calls the `dispose()` method from this observable (remember the `create()` and `createWithDisposable()` functions to create an observable).

The `Disposable` class also gives us functions to control groups of `Disposable` objects. The two most important types of Disposable are **CompositeDisposable** and **RefCountDisposable**.

A `CompositeDisposable()` object wraps other Disposables. So when you call the `dispose()` method of the parent object, it will call dispose for all children. You can see this behavior in this example:

```
var firstDisposable = Rx.Disposable
        .create(()=>console.log('disposing first'));
var secondDisposable = Rx.Disposable
        .create(()=>console.log('disposing second'));

var composite = new
Rx.CompositeDisposable(firstDisposable,secondDisposable);

composite.dispose();
```

In this example, we create two Disposable objects (`firstDisposable` and `secondDisposable`) and wrap them under `CompositeDisposable()` (composite). So when we call the `dispose()` method of the `CompositeDisposable()` object (composite), it will call the `dispose()` method of the two children as well (`firstDisposable` and `secondDisposable`).

If you run this code, you will see the following output:

```
disposing first
disposing second
```

The `RefCountDisposable` object does the opposite. It takes a `Disposable` object and lets you distribute references to this Disposable (using the `getDisposable()` method) but protects it from being disposed unless all the references already have been disposed. This is really useful to manage resources being used by multiple Observables/Observers.

This code shows a `RefCountDisposable` usage:

```javascript
var disposable = Rx.Disposable.create(function () {
    console.log('releasing connection');
});

var refCountDisposable = new Rx.RefCountDisposable(disposable);

var firstDisposable = refCountDisposable.getDisposable();
var secondDisposable = refCountDisposable.getDisposable();

firstDisposable.dispose();
secondDisposable.dispose();

console.log('first and second disposed. Disposing refCount');

refCountDisposable.dispose();
```

If you run this code, you will see the following output:

```
first and second disposed. Disposing refCount
releasing connection
```

The output shows that we need to dispose everything to dispose the `RefCountDisposable` children.

 Disposables are an important feature to enhance the control of the life cycle of your resources.

RxJS Schedulers

Schedulers are used to determine where a task is going to be executed (current thread, thread pool, and so on).

You can use them to run any type of task that you want, but RxJS Observables use schedulers to propagate data. For this reason, you can optionally define a Scheduler when creating a new Observable.

As you might expect, having control of which execution context you task should run in (or your Observable should process elements in) is specially useful when you are running in a multithread environment.

 As RxJS runs in a single-thread environment, other than the default settings, you should be really cautious when using a scheduler to propagate data from an Observable. Incorrect use can block your thread.

Summary

In this chapter, you learned the basics of functional reactive programming using RxJS, and it became clear that it is a more extensive framework.

We started to use different objects such as Observables, Observers, Subjects, Disposables, and Schedulers.

Some of these concepts don't even exist in the bacon.js world, and they give us more power over our code.

With Subjects, you learned how to create an Observable using a push style.

With Disposable, you gained more control over the life cycle of your code, as it lets you tear down your resources gracefully.

With Schedulers, you learned that if you want, you can control in which context your code will be executed, giving you more power over how Observables would propagate data. You also learned the importance of avoiding schedulers, other than the default ones, when using RxJS.

In the next chapter, we will use our first operators to transform data, as we did in the previous chapter using bacon.js. Once again, we will see how it can lead to cleaner, more readable, and testable code. The operators discussed in the next chapter are the most important ones; along with Observables and Observers, they construct the foundations of functional reactive programming.

If you are using libraries such as `lodash` or `underscore` or if you are up to date with the new methods of Array in JavaScript, you probably have already used some of the operators discussed in the next chapter. This includes the `map()`, `flatMap()`, `filter()`, and `reduce()` operators.

4
Transforming Data - Map, Filter, and Reduce

In the previous chapter, we started discussing the use of RxJS in our programs. To start using it, we compared Observables in Reactive Extensions with EventStreams and Properties in bacon.js. Then we looked at some of the most common sources of data we can use to create Observables, as follows:

- Arrays
- Range
- Interval
- Promises and callbacks
- DOM events
- Any arbitrary source

After this initial overview of the RxJS API on how to create Observables, we learned how to subscribe to them so we are able to take action whenever new data is made available in the Observable. Subscribing to an Observable means being able to not only react to new incoming data, but also to take some action when an error occurs or an Observable finishes. To do this, we learned how to use the `subscribe()` method, using functions or by creating an Observer.

We also learned how to use Subjects. Subjects allow us to create new Observables and keep pushing data to them.

RxJS gives us a lot more control of the life cycle of our Observables and even our application. Also, in the previous chapter, we used Disposables and Schedulers. They let us perform a teardown of our objects and control how we publish items in our Observable sequences.

With all of the knowledge we have gathered, so far we are now ready to add operators to our observables and make them more reusable and testable.

In this chapter, we will have a look at the four operators that are the backbone of any functional reactive program. They are as follows:

- `map()`
- `flatMap()`
- `filter()`
- `reduce()`

These are the most widely used/important operators. This chapter will be filled with lots of examples that will help you understand the usage of these operators. If you learn them well, they will make your road through functional reactive programming a lot easier, enabling you to learn about more specific operators and also how you can combine operators.

In this chapter, you will learn the following topics:

- Adding operators to Observables
- Using the `map()` and `flatMap()` operators
- Using the `filter()` operator
- Using the `reduce()` operator

Adding operators to observables

In Chapter 2, *Reacting for the First Time*, we used operators using bacon.js. They let us transform our data before it reaches the subscribers of the given Observable. The operators in RxJS work similar to the ones in bacon.js; some even have the same name. They are just methods called from Observable objects, as you can see in the following example:

```
Rx.Observable
  .just('Hello ')
  .map((msg)=>msg+'World')
  .subscribe((msg)=> console.log(msg));
```

In this example, we created an Observable, which emits only one string, and called the map() operator over this Observable and subscribed to it to show the result in the console:

Hello World

> If you can't recall the map() operator from Chapter 2, *Reacting for the First Time*, don't worry! We will see more of it and what it does later in this chapter.

Every time you call an operator over an observable, it returns a new observable with the transformation applied. This way, we can chain multiples operators easily, as follows:

```
Rx.Observable
    .of(1,2,3)
    .map((num)=>num*2)
    .filter((num)=> num>2)
    .subscribe((num)=>console.log(num));
```

In the preceding example, we created an Observable that emits three numbers. Then we called the map() operator over this Observable to first transform data and then apply the filter() operator to generate a new Observable. This code can also be written in the following way:

```
var initialObservable = Rx.Observable.of(1,2,3);
var initialMappedObservable = initialObservable
        .map((num)=>num*2);
var initialMappedAndFilteredObservable = initialMappedObservable
        .filter((num)=> num>2);
initialMappedAndFilteredObservable.subscribe((num)=>console.log(num));
```

Both provide the same output when executed:

```
4
6
```

Each of the Observables that is created after you apply an operator can be subscribed to, increasing the reuse of your code. Using operators, we can write cleaner and more testable code as it lets us detach the origin of our data from what to do with the data.

The map() operator

The `map()` operator is common when working with arrays or any other kinds of sequences in functional languages and frameworks. In JavaScript, array objects have a method called `map()`. This method is available in all modern browsers now.

The `map()` operator calls the provided function once for each element in the Observable. This function takes the object in the Observable as input and returns another object. So the Observable returned by the `map()` operator will propagate the result of calling the map function for each element of the original Observable.

The provided function is called as soon as the object is propagated by the original Observable; it is called in the same order.

So the `map()` operator has the following signature:

```
observable.map(mapFunction, [thisContext]);
```

The first parameter is mandatory and the second is optional:

- `mapFunction`: This is a function that takes an element of the observable as input and returns another object to be propagated instead
- `thisContext`: This is any object to be used as the `this` (JavaScript context) of `mapFunction`

If we have an Observable of numbers and want to create a new Observable by doubling these numbers, we can use the `map()` operator, as follows:

```
Rx.Observable
    .of(1,2,3)
    .map((i)=>i*2)
    .subscribe((i)=>console.log(i));
```

In this code, first we created an Observable that propagated three numbers (1, 2, and 3). Then, we applied the `map()` operator over this Observable; this created a new Observable with the mapped objects. Then we subscribed to this Observable to log all the elements. If you run the preceding code, you will see this output in your console:

```
2
4
6
```

This operation can be represented by the following diagram:

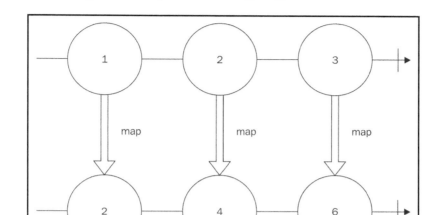

This operator can be used over any kind of object, and as described in this chapter, it doesn't change the initial Observable and always creates a new Observable:

```
var namesObservable = Rx.Observable.of("John","Mary")

var helloObservable = namesObservable.map((name)=>"Hello "+name)
helloObservable.subscribe((i)=>console.log(i));

var thanksObservable = namesObservable.map((name)=>name+" thanks for your visit.")
thanksObservable.subscribe((i)=>console.log(i));
```

In the preceding code, we created an Observable from two usernames (John and Mary). We then mapped it to an Observable of a string saying hello to each user, and we subscribed to the observable to print each message in the console.We also created a new Observable for a different message using the original Observable (with only the names), then we subscribed to it to log the message. If you run the preceding code, you will be presented with following output:

```
Hello John
Hello Mary
John thanks for your visit.
Mary thanks for your visit.
```

There is an alias for this operator called `select`.

The flatMap() operator

In the previous section, we saw the `map()` operator and how we can use it to map an object into another object in an observable. The `flatMap()` operator works similarly. It receives a function as a parameter. The function provided as argument must returns an Observable, and the elements of this Observable is propagated instead.

This operator may seen a little bit confusing, but there is another way to understand it. The `flatMap()` operator runs the given function for each element in the original array. It creates an Observable that will emit each piece of data coming out from other Observables keeping the order.

The `flatMap()` operator is illustrated in the following signature:

```
observable.flatMap(flatMapFunction, [thisContext]);
```

The first parameter is mandatory and the second is optional:

- `flatMapFunction`: This is a function that takes an element of the observable as input and returns another observable whose elements are going to be propagated instead
- `thisContext`: This is any object to be used as the `this` (JavaScript context) of `flatMapFunction`

You can see an example usage of this operator in the following code:

```
Rx.Observable
    .of(1,2,3)
    .flatMap((i)=>Rx.Observable.of(i,i*2))
    .subscribe((i)=>console.log(i));
```

In the preceding example, we first create an Observable that will propagate three numbers (1, 2, and 3). Then, we apply the `flatMap()` operator over this Observable; this will create a new Observable that will emit each value emitted by each Observable, and it will be returned by the `flatMapFunction`. The `flatMapFunction` returns an Observable containing the value and its double. So in the value 1 example, we create an Observable emitting the values 1 and 2; for value 2, we emit 2 and 4; and for value 3, we emit 3 and 6.

If we run the preceding code, it will display this output:

```
1
2
2
4
3
6
```

This operation can be represented by the following diagram:

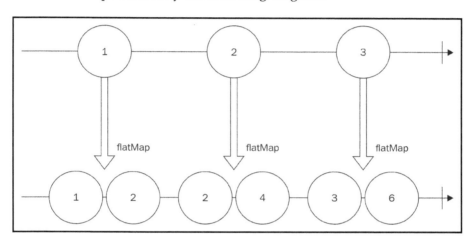

We can chain different operators easily, as follows:

```
Rx.Observable
    .of(1,2,3)
    .map((i)=>i+1)
    .flatMap((i)=>Rx.Observable.of(i,i*2))
    .subscribe((i)=>console.log(i));
```

In the preceding example, we chained the map() and flatMap() operators. First we create an Observable for 1, 2, and 3, then we use the map() operator to add 1 to each value (now we have an Observable with values 2, 3, and 4). Then, we use the flatMap() operator to emit a new sequence containing the value and its double.

If you run the preceding code, you will see following output:

```
2
4
3
6
4
8
```

 There is an alias for this operator called `selectMany`.

The filter() operator

The `filter()` operator lets you create a new Observable after omitting some of the data from the original Observable. It receives a function as argument that is called for each element in the original Observable, and it must return an either true or false (actually it can be any truthy or falsy value). If the result of the execution of `filterFunction` for an object is true, then this object will be propagated; otherwise, it will be omitted.

The `filter()` operator has the following signature:

```
observable.filter(filterFunction, [thisContext]);
```

The first parameter is mandatory and the second is optional:

- `filterFunction`: This is a function that takes an element of the observable as input and returns any truthy or falsy value. If the result of the execution of this function for a given object is true, then this object is propagated; otherwise, it is omitted.
- `thisContext`: This is any object to be used as the `thisContext` of `flatMapFunction`

We can see an example of the usage of `filter()` as follows:

```
Rx.Observable
    .of(1,2,3)
    .filter((i)=> i % 2 === 1 )
    .subscribe((i)=>console.log(i));
```

In the preceding example, we first create an Observable that will propagate three numbers (1, 2, and 3). Then, we apply the `filter()` operator over this Observable; this will create a new Observable that will emit only the value i, where i `%2 === 1`. So the new Observable propagates only odd numbers.

If you run the preceding code, you will see this output:

```
1
3
```

This operation can be represented by the following diagram as well:

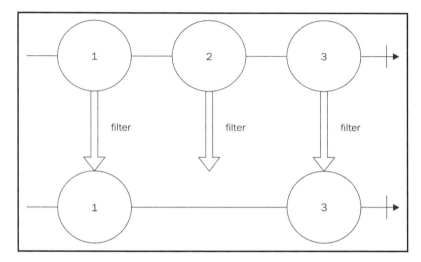

In this example, we are always returning true or false, but we can also return any truthy or falsy value.

 A truthy value is any object that acts true when evaluated as a Boolean. Falsy values are those that act false when evaluated as a Boolean.

Falsy values are as follows:

- False
- 0
- ""(empty string)
- Null
- Undefined
- NaN

All other values available in JavaScript are truthy values.

The following is an example that filters an Observable for only truthy values:

```
Rx.Observable
    .of(0,1,"hello",null,"")
    .filter((i)=> i )
    .subscribe((i)=>console.log(i));
```

If you run the preceding code, you will see this output:

```
1
hello
```

 There is an alias for this operator called `where`.

The reduce() operator

The `reduce()` operator lets you run a function to accumulate all the values of an Observable to generate a new Observable containing only one value (the accumulated value).

This operator has the following signature:

```
observable.reduce(accumulatorFunction, [initialValue]);
```

The first parameter is optional and the second one is mandatory:

- accumulatorFunction: This is a function that is used to accumulate values from an observable. This function can receive up to four parameters:
  - acc: This is an accumulated value
  - currentValue: This is the value used in this iteration
  - currentIndex: This is a zero-based index of this iteration
  - source: This is the observable used
- initialValue: This is the initial accumulator

We can use this function to sum up all the values in an Observable containing numbers, as follows:

```
Rx.Observable
    .of(1,2,3)
    .reduce((acc,current)=>acc+current)
    .subscribe((i)=>console.log(i));
```

In this example, we first create an Observable that will propagate three numbers (1, 2, and 3). Then, we apply the reduce() operator over this Observable; this will create a new Observable with only one value, and the value will be the sum of each element in this sequence.

This method runs in the following iteration:

1. If an initial value is supplied, we use it as the accumulator and the first element in the sequence as the current value; if not, we use the first element in the sequence as the accumulator and the second as the current value.
2. Run accumulatorFunction for the accumulator and the current value.
3. Set the current value as the next element in the sequence.
4. Go back to *step 2* until you process the whole list.

So if you run the preceding code, you will see following output:

6

This operation can be represented by the following diagram:

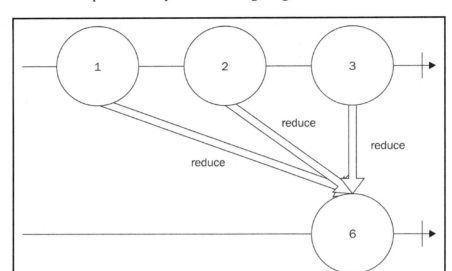

We can also supply an initial value for the `reduce()` operator, as can be seen in the following example:

```
Rx.Observable
    .of("w","o","r","l","d")
    .reduce((acc,current)=>acc+current, "Hello ")
    .subscribe((i)=>console.log(i));
```

As you can imagine, running this code will concatenate the whole string so you could see the following message on your console:

```
Hello world
```

Summary

In this chapter, we learned how to apply operators to observables. This helps decouple our code and improve its testability and readability. This is the first time we used the following operators in RxJS such as `map()`, `flatMap()`, `filter()`, and `reduce()`.

These are the most widely used operators in RxJS, and for this reason, they are also the most important ones. We used some of them in bacon.js, but in this chapter, we were able to have a more in-depth look at each one of them; diagrams and examples only helped us understand their usage better.

In the next chapter, we will talk about the problem of backpressure on observables and which actions we can take to mitigate this problem. We will also learn more about operators to filter data from observables.

5
The World Changes Too Fast - Operators to Deal with Backpressure

In the last chapter, we learned how we can use an operator to transform the data emitted by an observable, and also how we can chain this operator, making it reusable as each operator creates a new observable which can be used by multiple observers.

We learned how we can use the following four different operators:

- `map()`
- `flatMap()`
- `filter()`
- `reduce()`

These operators are the most important and most used in functional reactive programming. We saw examples and diagrams to make sure we understood how we can use these operators.

The usage of these operators goes beyond the last chapter. We will keep using them through the whole book, and we will use them heavily in the last two chapters, since we will create a client and server for a real-time web chat using functional reactive programming (with the `RxJS` library)

In this chapter, we will cover a common problem in programs and how we can mitigate it using functional reactive programming operators. This problem is called **backpressure**. We will also cover more operators to filter data from our observables.

In this chapter, we will cover the following topics:

- What is backpressure?
- How can we mitigate backpressure using RxJS?
- Lossy strategies to deal with backpressure
- Loss-less strategies to deal with backpressure
- Buffering observables
- Pausing observables
- Operators to deal with backpressure
- Operators to filter data

What is backpressure?

When using functional reactive programming, we model our problems using streams of data or events (called observables), which can be transformed (using operators) and eventually will cause some effect (through an observer). Now imagine that we have an observable which emits data faster than our observer can process; this will lead to a problem called backpressure.

This problem can also happen when we want to keep an observable running at a certain pace. Imagine that you want to log in to the console all the tweets from a certain hashtag, but you want to log at most one each for a few seconds to make sure the user can read the tweets. This also can lead to backpressure if the hashtags have more tweets per second than a human is capable of reading.

Using RxJS, we have two possible strategies to deal with this problem.

We can discard some data. You might not be interested in all the movements of your user mouse or all the tweets from a certain hashtag. You are only interested in the big picture.

You can keep queuing the data until you are capable of process it or process it in a batch.

Common strategies to deal with backpressure

In RxJS we have several operators which can be used to mitigate the backpressure problem, they belong to two different family of strategies the lossy and the loss-less strategies. We will see each one in detail in this chapter.

Lossy strategies to deal with backpressure

Lossy strategies to deal with backpressure are the ones we must use when we want to discard some data. As we discussed, you might not be interested in all the movements from your user mouse.

 Lossy strategies let you mitigate the problem of backpressure using constant memory, as we don't keep any buffers.

The throttle() operator

The first lossy technique to deal with backpressure is the `throttle()` operator. This operator lets you propagate the elements emitted by the observable at a certain interval.

This operator is perfect for implementing rate limiting, such as the problem of showing tweets as fast as a human can read.

The `throttle()` operator has the following signature:

```
observable.throttle(interval, [scheduler]);
```

The first parameter is mandatory and the second is optional:

- `interval`: This is the time interval, in milliseconds, between the emission of data
- `scheduler`: This is used to propagate the data

The easiest way to show the usage of this operator is to apply it on an observable that already emits elements at a certain rate. We can use the `throttle()` method to further limit this rate and verify the response. We can do this by creating an `Observable` with the `interval()` method, as shown in the following example:

```
Rx.Observable
    .interval(50)
    .subscribe((i)=>console.log(i));
```

If you run this example, you will see a lot of number being printed really fast in your console:

```
0
1
2
3
//continues printing until you stop the program
```

But we can use the `throttle()` operator to control the rate of the output. Using this method, we will also discard some of our data, and for this reason, we won't see the output in all the numbers being printed:

```
Rx.Observable
    .interval(50)
    .throttle(1000)
    .subscribe((i)=>console.log(i));
```

If you run this code, you will see an output as follows:

```
0
18
37
//continues printing until you stop the program
```

The numbers printed in the console may vary in different executions.

This operation is illustrated in the following diagram:

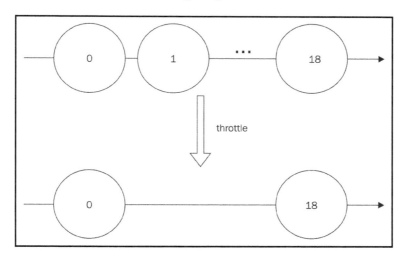

In this example, we are using an infinite sequence. Now let's test this operator in a finite observable and also apply it to a subject (so we don't forget how we use subjects):

```
var subject = new Rx.Subject();

var throttledObserver = subject.throttle(50);

throttledObserver.subscribe(
    (i)=>console.log(i),
    (err)=>console.log(err),
    ()=>console.log('Finished')
);

subject.onNext(0);
subject.onNext(1);

setTimeout(()=>{
    subject.onNext(2);
    subject.onNext(3);
    subject.onCompleted();
},200);
```

In the preceding code, we first create a `subject`. We then call the `throttle()` operator, to receive the data on the given maximum rate of one every 50 milliseconds, and we `subscribe` to it (for data, error, and completion). Then we push the data into our `subject`. If we run this code, we will see the following output:

```
0
2
Finished
```

The `throttle()` method will first propagate the first element in the observable (the number 0) and the second element (the number 1) will be discarded (as we did not elapse the 50 milliseconds interval). We only have new data available after 200 milliseconds and we will propagate it (the number 2) because we already waited for more than 50 milliseconds since our last data propagated (the number 0). We will then push the last element in the `subject` (the number 3), which is discarded (less than 50 milliseconds since our last emission, the number 2) and we finally finish the `subject`.

The sample() operator

The `sample()` operator can also be used to mitigate the problem of backpressure in a lossy way. It lets you receive data from the observable at every given interval.

The `sample()` operator has the following signature:

```
observable.sample(interval, [scheduler]);
```

The first parameter is mandatory and the second is optional:

- `interval`: This is the time interval, in milliseconds, between the emission of data. This parameter can also be an `observable`. In this case, this `observable` will be used to sample the data.
- `scheduler`: This is used to propagate the data

Let's use the same example from the `throttle()` method (using the `interval()` method to create an `Observable`) and change it to use the `sample()` method:

```
Rx.Observable
    .interval(50)
    .sample(1000)
    .subscribe((i)=>console.log(i));
```

If you run this code, you will see an output as follows:

```
18
37
//continues printing until you stop the program
```

 The numbers printed in the console may vary in different executions.

This operation is illustrated in the following diagram:

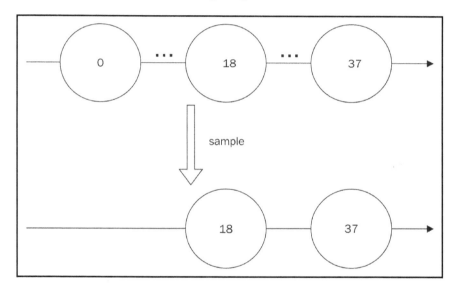

We can also modify this code to use a `sample()` observable instead of a number:

```
Rx.Observable
    .interval(50)
    .sample(Rx.Observable.interval(1000))
    .subscribe((i)=>console.log(i));
```

Running this code will print the same output as the previous one.

This code is slightly changed from another example from the `throttle()` method:

```
var subject = new Rx.Subject();
var sampledObserver = subject.sample(50);

sampledObserver.subscribe(
    (i)=>console.log(i),
    (err)=>console.log(err),
    ()=>console.log('Finished')
);
subject.onNext(0);
subject.onNext(1);

setTimeout((()=>{
    subject.onNext(2);
    subject.onNext(3);
    subject.onCompleted();
},200);
```

If you run this code, you will see the following output:

```
1
3
Finished
```

This happens because the `sample()` operator will wait 50 milliseconds and send the last emitted data (the number 1). After more than 50 milliseconds have elapsed, no data is emitted, so it doesn't propagate any data. After 200 milliseconds, we push two numbers in the `subject` (2 and 3) and complete it, so the `sample()` method will propagate the last (the number 3) and finishes.

The debounce() operator

The next lossy technique for backpressure is the usage of the `debounce()` operator. This operator emits data from the observable only after a certain interval when the last emission from this observable has passed.

This method is really useful to implement features such as search-as-you-type, as we might not want to call our server for every keystroke from the user. Using this method, we can let the user keep typing and search only when the user stays a few milliseconds without typing anything.

The `debounce()` operator has the following signature:

```
observable.debounce(interval, [scheduler]);
```

The first parameter is mandatory and the second is optional:

- `interval`: This is the time to wait in milliseconds
- `scheduler`: This is used to propagate the data

The first example for the `throttle()` operator uses an `Observable` created from an `interval()`. Now let's change that example to use the `debounce()` operator instead:

```
Rx.Observable
    .interval(50)
    .debounce(1000)
    .subscribe((i)=>console.log(i));
```

If you run this code, you will see nothing printed in the console because the `Observable` never stays `1000` milliseconds without emitting a value, but let's assume we can debounce `10` instead of `1000` as follows:

```
Rx.Observable
    .interval(50)
    .debounce(10)
    .subscribe((i)=>console.log(i));
```

In this case, you will see this printed in your console:

```
0
1
2
3
//continues printing until you stop the program.
```

This operation is illustrated in the following diagram:

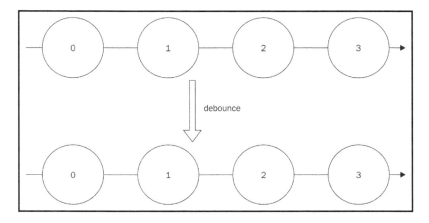

Now let's see the example we discussed about a user typing too fast. Let's check the following example:

```html
<html>
<head></head>
<body>

<input type="text" id="my_input"/>

<ul id="my_ul"></ul>

<script
src="https://cdnjs.cloudflare.com/ajax/libs/rxjs/4.1.0/rx.all.js"></script>

<script>
Rx.Observable
        .fromEvent(document.getElementById("my_input"),"keyup")
        .map(function(e){return e.target.value;})
        .debounce(200)
        .subscribe(function(text){
            var node = document.createElement("li");
            var textnode=document.createTextNode("CALLING THE SERVER WITH
==> "+text);
            node.appendChild(textnode);
            document.getElementById('my_ul').appendChild(node);
        });
</script>
</body>
</html>
```

In this example, we create an HTML page with a text input, a `ul`, to show the moments we are running our `subscribe()` function, and add the RxJS library as a dependency. Then we have a script block with our script.

In this script, we first create an `Observable` for every `keyup` event in the input text, We map this event to the value of the input text (the text we typed), as we don't want to run the subscription for every keystroke. We will debounce it for 200 milliseconds, so we only call the observer if we stay more than 200 milliseconds without typing in the input text. Our observer creates a `li` with the text to be used in the search. As we don't have any API to call, we will only add this to the page.

This is illustrated in the following screenshot:

```
some search

    • CALLING THE SERVER WITH ==> som
    • CALLING THE SERVER WITH ==> some
    • CALLING THE SERVER WITH ==> some s
    • CALLING THE SERVER WITH ==> some scar
    • CALLING THE SERVER WITH ==> some search
```

The pausable() observables

The last operator to implement the lossy technique to deal with backpressure is the
pausable() operator. This operator returns a pausable() observable so we can pause it
(and discard all the data while paused) and resume it when we are ready to accept more
data.

The pausable() method has the following signature:

```
observable.pausable();
```

As you can see, it doesn't accept any parameter.

We can see an example of the usage of this operator in the following code:

```
var pausableObservable = Rx.Observable
    .interval(50)
    .pausable();
pausableObservable.subscribe((i)=>console.log(i));

pausableObservable.pause();

setTimeout(()=>{
    pausableObservable.resume();
},2000);
```

If you run this code, you will see the following output in your console:

```
0
1
2
3
//continues printing until you stop the program
```

In this example, we create an `Observable` which emits data every 50 milliseconds, but we pause it right after the subscription, so no data is emitted. Then after 2000 milliseconds, a function is called and we `resume` the observable, so it starts to print the data.

 This method works only with a hot observable. The observables created with the `interval()` method are cold observables and for this reason no data was discarded.

Now let's check this method in a `subject`:

```
var subject = new Rx.Subject();
var pausableObservable = subject.pausable();

pausableObservable.subscribe(
    (i)=>console.log(i),
    (err)=>console.log(err),
    ()=>console.log('Finished')
);

pausableObservable.pause();

subject.onNext(0);
subject.onNext(1);

setTimeout(()=>{
    subject.onNext(2);
    subject.onNext(3);
    subject.onCompleted();
},200);
setTimeout(()=>{
    pausableObservable.resume();
},2000);
```

We are using the same `subject` we used in all the examples in this session. The only change is that we `pause` it before we push any data and only `resume` it after all the data has been pushed, so if we run this code we will see this printed in the console:

Finished

All the data is discarded because the data was pushed while the observable was paused. This operation is illustrated in the following diagram:

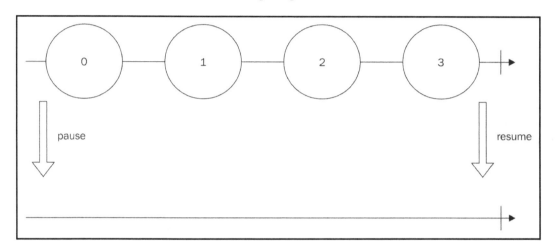

Loss-less operators to deal with backpressure

Loss-less strategies to deal with backpressure are the ones we must use when we can't afford losing data. If you are using them to show messages in a web chat, you might want to `buffer` them.

 Be careful when using loss-less strategies to mitigate the problem of backpressure as this increases the memory your program will need.

Buffering

The first loss-less technique to deal with backpressure is using a `buffer` to store the data, so we can process it in a batch.

All methods for buffering data start with `buffer` in the name (here we will learn `bufferWithCount()`, `bufferWithTime()`, and `bufferWithTimeOrCount()`), and basically they will store data in memory until the `buffer` is fulfilled and propagates an array containing the data.

If an error message is propagated by the observable, this message will be sent immediately without first emitting the `buffer`, even if the `buffer` contains data.

The bufferWithCount() operator

The first method to `buffer` data is `bufferWithCount()`. The `bufferWithCount()` method lets you specify the size of the `buffer`. With this method, the data will be stored in an array until the size of this array reaches the given count, upon which this array is propagated.

The `bufferWithCount()` method has the following signature:

```
observable.bufferWithCount(size, [skip]);
```

The first parameter is mandatory and the second is optional:

- `size`: This is a number specifying the size of the `buffer`.
- `skip`: This is a number specifying how many items we should skip to create the next `buffer`. If not provided, it defaults to the `size` (this way the next `buffer` will contain only new elements).

Now let's see an example of this method:

```
Rx.Observable
    .interval(50)
    .bufferWithCount(2)
    .subscribe((arr)=>console.log(arr));
```

In this example, we first create an `Observable` from an interval of 50 milliseconds. We then use the `bufferWithCount()` method to `buffer` it in chunks of 10, and finally we print it to the console.

If you run this code, you will see the following output:

```
[ 0, 1]
[2, 3]
//continues printing until you stop the program
```

This operation is illustrated in the following diagram:

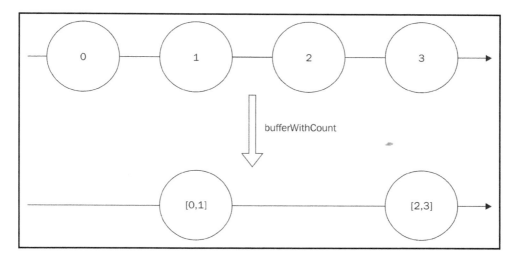

Now let's see what happens if an error is propagated in our `buffer`. For this, let's create a `subject`:

```
var subject = new Rx.Subject();

var bufferedObservable = subject.bufferWithCount(2);

bufferedObservable.subscribe(
    (i)=>console.log(i),
    (err)=>console.log('An error happened ' + err.message),
    ()=>console.log('Finished')
);

subject.onNext(0);
subject.onNext(1);
subject.onNext(2);

subject.onError(new Error(':('));

subject.onNext(3);
subject.onCompleted();
```

In this example, we first create a `subject` and use the `bufferWithCount()` to create chunks of two items and subscribe to it. We then push three values (0, 1, and 2). The first two (0 and 1) will be propagated and printed in the console, the third is buffered, until an error is pushed into the `subject`. This makes the error go directly through the observable.

If you run this code, you will see the following output:

```
[ 0, 1 ]
An error happened :(
```

Now, you might be wondering what happens if an `observable` finish and the count doesn't reach the desired count. To test it, we can use a simple program:

```
Rx.Observable
    .of(0,1,2,3,4)
    .bufferWithCount(2)
    .subscribe((i)=> console.log(i));
```

If you run this code, you will see the following output:

```
[ 0, 1 ]
[ 2, 3 ]
[ 4 ]
```

So, as you can see, if the original `observable` finishes, RxJS will flush the current `buffer`.

Let's see now how the second parameter works, comparing the two subscriptions:

```
var observable = Rx.Observable.interval(1000);

var observableWithDefaultSkip = observable.bufferWithCount(4);
var observableWithSkipOne = observable.bufferWithCount(4,1);

observableWithDefaultSkip.subscribe((arr)=>console.log('with default skip
:'+arr));
observableWithSkipOne.subscribe(
    (arr)=>console.log('with default skip equals to one:'+arr)
);
```

If you run this code (and wait a little bit), you will see an output as follows:

```
with default skip :0,1,2,3
with default skip equals to one:0,1,2,3
with default skip equals to one:1,2,3,4
with default skip equals to one:2,3,4,5
with default skip equals to one:3,4,5,6
with default skip :4,5,6,7
with default skip equals to one:4,5,6,7
//continues printing until you stop the program
```

As you can see by the output, if you don't provide the skip value, the `buffer` is basically erased after being propagated. This way it runs only every 4 seconds (as our original `observable` pushes the value every second, it takes 4 seconds to fill four items in the array), but if you provide a skip value, it will remove this amount of items (from left to right) and always push new values in the end of the array. This way it runs every second (because our `buffer` always keeps three items from the last `buffer`, it takes only 1 second to fill the array).

And finally, one useful application of the `bufferWithCount()` method is to calculate the average of the last *X* numbers in the sequence. To show this application, let's first create an `Observable` to generate random numbers:

```
var randomNumbersGenerator = Rx.Observable
        .interval(100)
        .map((i)=>Math.floor(Math.random()*100));
```

Here we create an `Observable` to generate items every `100` milliseconds. We then map it to an integer value between `0` and `99`.

Now let's calculate the average of the last five items. To do this, we call the `bufferWithCount()` method with a size of `5` and skip `1`. Then we calculate the average and print in the console.

The full code is as follows:

```
var randomNumbersObservable = Rx.Observable
        .interval(100)
        .map((i)=>Math.floor(Math.random()*100));

randomNumbersObservable
    .bufferWithCount(5,1)
    .map((arr)=>{
        var sum = arr.reduce((acc,b)=>acc+b);
        return sum/arr.length;
    })
.subscribe((i)=>console.log('The average of the last five items is: '+i));
```

If you run this code, you will see an output as follows (the value may vary on different executions of the program):

```
The average of the last five items is: 54.8
The average of the last five items is: 60.6
The average of the last five items is: 62.6
//... continues printing until you stop the program
```

The bufferWithTime() operator

The next operator to `buffer` data lets you `buffer` data for a certain amount of time. It's called `bufferWithTime()`. This operator will store data in an array until a given time is elapsed.

The `bufferWithTime()` method has the following signature:

```
observable.bufferWithTime(time, [skipTime], [scheduler]);
```

The first parameter is mandatory and the other two are optional:

- `time`: This is the time in milliseconds to `buffer` the data, before propagating it
- `skipTime`: This is similar to the skip parameter in the `bufferWithCount()`, but it is the time in milliseconds to skip
- `scheduler`: This is used to propagate data

An example of the usage of this method is as follows:

```
Rx.Observable
    .interval(100)
    .bufferWithTime(210)
    .subscribe((arr)=>console.log(arr));
```

It creates an `Observable` from an `interval()`, `buffers` the data for `1000` milliseconds, and then uses `subscribe()` to log it in the console.

Running this code, you will see the following output:

```
[ 0, 1 ]
[ 2, 3 ]
[ 4, 5 ]
//continues printing until you stop the program
```

This operation is illustrated in the following diagram:

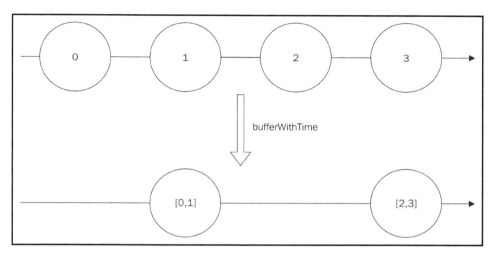

Now, you might be wondering what happens if the time elapsed and no data sent by the original observable; you have two valid guesses:

- No data is propagated
- An empty array is propagated

To test it, let's create an `Observable` from an `interval()` and `filter()` it so only a few elements are propagated:

```
Rx.Observable
    .interval(50)
    .filter((i)=>i<10)
    .bufferWithTime(150)
    .subscribe((arr)=>console.log(arr));
```

If we run this code, we will see the following output:

```
[ 0, 1 ]
[ 2, 3, 4 ]
[ 5, 6, 7 ]
[ 8, 9 ]
[]
[]
[]
//keeps printing empty array
```

So, looking at the output in the console, it is easy to see the right answer: an empty array is propagated.

We can also change the last example from the `bufferWithCount()` operator, to calculate the average from the numbers in the last 5 seconds every second. To do this, all we have to do is to use the operator `bufferWithTime()` and adjust the time and `skipTime` parameters:

```
var randomNumbersObservable = Rx.Observable
      .interval(100)
      .map((i)=>Math.floor(Math.random()*100));

randomNumbersObservable
    .bufferWithTime(5000,1000)
    .map((arr)=>{
    var sum = arr.reduce((acc,b)=>acc+b);
    return sum/arr.length;
})
.subscribe((i)=>console.log('The average of the last five second is: '+i));
```

As you can see, we changed the operator `bufferWithCount()` to use the `bufferWithTime()`. We will `buffer` for 5000 milliseconds and use a window of 1000 milliseconds, and also change the message to be printed in the console , as now we show `The average of the last five seconds` instead of the last five items.

If you run this code, you will see an output as follows:

```
The average of the last five seconds is: 48.875
The average of the last five seconds is: 50.08163265306123
The average of the last five seconds is: 49.61224489795919
The average of the last five seconds is: 49.3125
//continues printing until you stop the program
```

The bufferWithTimeOrCount() operator

The last operator to `buffer` data we will see is the `bufferWithTimeOrCount()` operator. In the last two sessions, we learned about the `bufferWithCount()` operator which lets us put a limit on the size of the array, and the `bufferWithTime()` operator which lets us put a limit on the time to fill the `buffer`. Sometimes we might want to put a maximum on both.

The `bufferWithTimeOrCount()` method has the following signature:

```
observable.bufferWithTimeOrCount(time,count,[scheduler]);
```

The two first parameter are mandatory and the last is optional:

- `time`: This is the time in milliseconds to `buffer` the data, before propagating it
- `count`: This is the maximum size of the `buffer`
- `scheduler`: This is used to propagate the data

We can use the same example from the other `buffer` operators to see this operator in action:

```
Rx.Observable
    .interval(100)
    .bufferWithTimeOrCount(1000,5)
    .subscribe((arr)=>console.log(arr));
```

In this example, we will always limit based in the count (as in the time span of `1000` milliseconds, we generate more than `5` items on the `Observable`), so running this code, we will see the following output:

```
[ 0, 1, 2, 3, 4 ]
[ 5, 6, 7, 8, 9 ]
[ 10, 11, 12, 13, 14 ]
[ 15, 16, 17, 18, 19 ]
//continues printing until you stop the program
```

But if we change the parameter using a smaller time, `150` milliseconds for instance, it will cap in the time:

```
Rx.Observable
    .interval(100)
    .bufferWithTimeOrCount(150,5)
    .subscribe((arr)=>console.log(arr));
```

The following output will be printed:

```
[ 0 ]
[ 1, 2 ]
[ 3 ]
[ 4, 5 ]
//continues printing until you stop the program
```

Those are basic examples. One cooler use of this operator is to detect triple clicks of the mouse in a DOM element.

Implementing this kind of behavior in Vanilla JS can be really messy, but it's really simple using RxJS:

```html
<html>
<head>
</head>
<body>
<span id="my_span">TRIPLE CLICK</span>
<ul id="my_ul"></ul>
<script
src="https://cdnjs.cloudflare.com/ajax/libs/rxjs/4.1.0/rx.all.js"></script>
<script>
    Rx.Observable
            .fromEvent(document.getElementById("my_span"),"click")
            .bufferWithTimeOrCount(1000,3)
            .filter(function(arr){
                return arr.length===3;
            })
            .subscribe(function(){
                var node = document.createElement("li");
                var textnode = document.createTextNode("TRIPLE CLICK
DETECTED");
                node.appendChild(textnode);
                document.getElementById('my_ul').appendChild(node);
            });
</script>
</body>
</html>
```

In this HTML page, we have a span where we will listen for triple clicks. For doing so, we create an `Observable` from the click events from it using the `fromEvent()` method, then we `buffer` the clicks for a second or three clicks (whatever happens first), as we want to detect triple clicks. We now filter the `Observable` to propagate only when the array size is equal to `3` (that's the case when we have a triple click), and finally we `subscribe` to add a `li` on the HTML page showing the span was clicked three times (now, try to implement the same behavior without functional reactive programming).

If you implement this example (and do some **TRIPLE CLICK** in the span), you will see a page as follows:

```
TRIPLE CLICK

  • TRIPLE CLICK DETECTED
  • TRIPLE CLICK DETECTED
  • TRIPLE CLICK DETECTED
  • TRIPLE CLICK DETECTED
  • TRIPLE CLICK DETECTED
```

Pausable observables (with buffer)

We already learned how to `pause` and `resume` observables in a lossy fashion; now we will see an operator to `pause` the observable and keep a `buffer` while paused so we don't lose any data.

The operator to `pause` and keep a `buffer` is called `pausableBuffered()`, and has the following signature:

```
observable.pausableBuffered();
```

As you can see, it doesn't accept any parameters.

We can see an example of the usage of this operator in the following code:

```
var pausableObservable = Rx.Observable
    .interval(500)
    .pausableBuffered();

pausableObservable.subscribe((i)=>console.log(i));

pausableObservable.pause();

setTimeout(()=>{
    pausableObservable.resume();
},4000);
```

In this example code, we create an `Observable` and call `pausableBuffered()` on it. We then `pause` it and wait `4000` milliseconds to `resume`. If you run this code, you will see the following output in your console:

```
0
1
2
3
4
//continues printing until you stop the program
```

Looking at the output, we can also notice that even being buffered, the data is always propagated one by one on `pausable` observables. This method also gives the programmer full control of when to stop and `resume` the observable.

Controlled observables

The last loss-less strategy to deal with backpressure we will see is the `controlled()` operator. This operator gives the programmer full control of buffers as it lets you `buffer` all data and request for the amount of data you want anytime.

This operator has the following signature:

```
observable.controlled();
```

As you can, see this method doesn't receive any parameters.

After creating a `controlled()` observable, you can use the method `request()` to request for a given number of items. The `request()` method has the following signature:

```
controlledObservable.request(count);
```

The parameter `count` is mandatory:

- `count`: This is the number of items to be pulled from the `Observable` (if absent, it defaults to zero).

An example usage of this method can be seen in following code:

```
var controllableObservable = Rx.Observable
    .interval(100)
    .controlled();

controllableObservable.subscribe((i)=>console.log(i));

controllableObservable.request(2);
setTimeout(()=>{
    console.log("Requesting more");
    controllableObservable.request(4);
},3000);
```

In this example, we create an `Observable` from an `interval()` and transform it to a `controlled()` observable with the `controlled()` method. Then we `subscribe` to it and request for two values (0 and 1 will be be printed in the console). We then wait for `3000` milliseconds and ask for four more items (2, 3, 4, and 5).

If you run this code, you will see the following output:

```
0
1
Requesting more
2
3
4
5
```

This operation is illustrated in the following diagram:

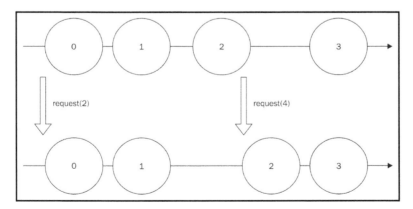

Now let's change our example to ask for more data than we have available in the
`Observable`:

```
var controllableObservable = Rx.Observable
    .of(0,1)
    .controlled();
controllableObservable.subscribe((i)=>console.log(i));
controllableObservable.request(3);
```

In this example, our `Observable` contains only two items (0 and 1) and we will request for
three items. If you run this code, you will see the following output:

```
0
1
```

So, if we ask for more data than we have available in our observable, it will just send all the
data that it has available.

This operation is illustrated in the following diagram:

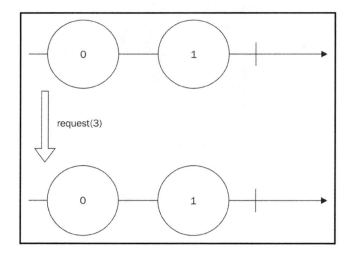

 The `controlled()` observable is a powerful tool as it gives the
programmer full control of when and how many items he wants.

For the last example, let's see what happens if an error is propagated in a `controlled()` observable:

```
var subject = new Rx.Subject();

var controlledObservable = subject.controlled();

controlledObservable.subscribe(
    (i)=>console.log(i),
    (err)=>console.log('An error happened ' + err.message),
    ()=>console.log('Finished')
);

subject.onNext(0);
subject.onNext(1);
subject.onNext(2);

subject.onError(new Error(':('));
subject.onNext(3);
subject.onCompleted();

controlledObservable.request(5);
```

Using a `subject`, we can easily push data into the stream. This `subject` is the same used throughout this chapter to push errors The only changes occur in the last line, where we request five items for our `controlled()` observable.

If you run this code, you will see the following output:

```
0
1
2
An error happened :(
```

Looking at the output, we see that the `controlled()` observable will pull the data (and run the observer) before the error happens and then propagates the error.

More ways to filter data

In RxJS, we also have other operators to filter data. In this section, we will learn about the following operators:

- `first()`
- `take()`

- `takeLast()`
- `takeWhile()`
- `skip()`
- `skipWhile()`

We can use these operators when we are interested only in a subset of data from an observable.

 There are other operators to filter data on RxJS but these are the most common ones.

The first() operator

The `first()` operator returns a new observable containing only the first element in an observable which satisfies a given condition. This operator has the following signature:

```
observable.first([condition],[context],[defaultValue]);
```

All parameters are optional:

- `condition`: This is the function which the value must satisfy to be retrieved
- `context`: This is an argument used in the given conditional function
- `defaultValue`: This is a value used as the default if the observable is exhausted and no item satisfies the given condition

If no condition is supplied, this operator returns the first element in the `Observable`. This is shown in the following example:

```
Rx.Observable
    .of(1,2,3)
    .first()
    .subscribe((i)=>console.log(i));
```

If you run this code, you will see the following output:

```
1
```

This operation is illustrated in the following diagram:

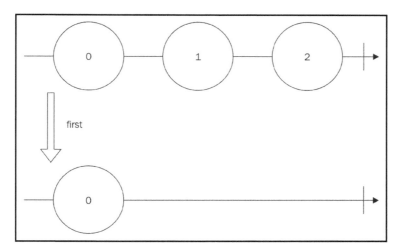

We can also supply a conditional function. In the following example, we will use the conditional function to retrieve the **first** even number on the `Observable`:

```
Rx.Observable
    .of(1,2,3)
    .first((i)=>i%2===0)
    .subscribe((i)=>console.log(i));
```

If you run this code, it will print the first even number in the observable, which is as follows:

2

We can also supply a default value if no element satisfies the condition:

```
var defaultValue = 'no even numbers';
Rx.Observable
    .of(1,3,5)
    .first((i)=>i%2===0,null,defaultValue)
    .subscribe((i)=>console.log(i));
```

Notice that we removed all even numbers from the observable, so when you run this code it will print the following:

no even numbers

The take() operator

This operator returns an `observable` containing a given number of contiguous data from the `observable`. It has the following signature:

```
observable.take(count, [scheduler]);
```

The first parameter is mandatory and the last is optional:

- `count`: This is the number of elements to be retrieved from the observable

- `scheduler`: This is used to deliver the `onCompleted()` method in the case of the count equaling `0`

The usage of this operator is really simple and can be seen in the following example:

```
Rx.Observable
    .of(1,3,5)
    .take(2)
    .subscribe((i)=>console.log(i));
```

In this example, we will take only the first two elements in the sequence, so running this code, we will see the following output:

```
1
3
```

This operation is illustrated in the following diagram:

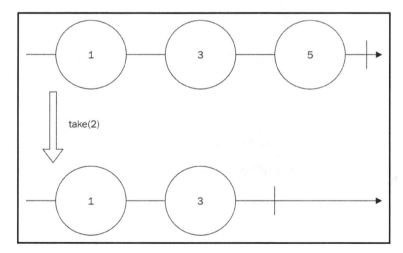

The takeLast() operator

The `takeLast()` operator is analogous to the `take()` operator. The only difference is it takes a given count from the end of the `observable`. It has the following signature:

```
observable.take(count);
```

The first parameter is mandatory:

- `count`: This is the number of elements to be retrieved from the end of the observable

We can change the example from the previous section to use this operator:

```
Rx.Observable
  .of(1,3,5)
  .takeLast(2)
  .subscribe((i)=>console.log(i));
```

In this code, the `takeLast()` operator generates a new `Observable` containing the last two elements in the original `Observable` (3 and 5), so, if you run this code, you will see the following output:

```
3
5
```

This operation is illustrated in the following diagram:

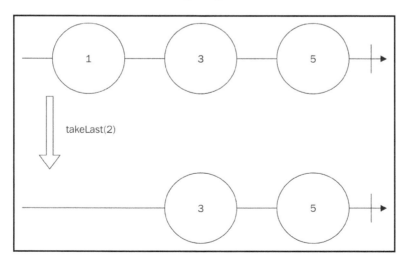

This operator keeps a `buffer` with the size needed to store the requested count of elements.

The takeWhile() operator

This is the last operator from the `take()` family we will see in this chapter. This operator lets you create an `observable` from the first contiguous sequence of elements in an `observable` satisfying a given conditional function. It has the following signature:

```
observable.takeWhile(condition, [context]);
```

The first parameter is mandatory and the last is optional:

- `condition`: This is a given function which the elements must satisfy
- `context`: This argument is used in the conditional function

We can use this operator to take the first contiguous sequence of even numbers, as can be seen in the following example:

```
Rx.Observable
    .of(2,4,5,6)
    .takeWhile((i)=>i%2===0)
    .subscribe((i)=>console.log(i));
```

In this code, we will test for even numbers. It will test from the beginning and stop when the first element doesn't satisfy the given condition. So, as the condition satisfies the first two numbers (2 and 4), but not the third number (5), it will print only the first two:

```
2
4
```

This operation is illustrated in the following diagram:

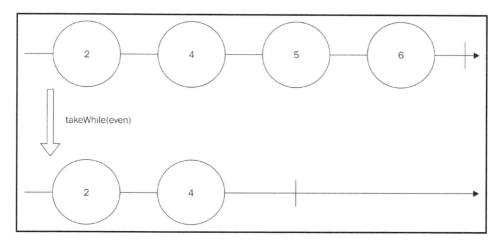

If the first element doesn't satisfy the condition, it will return an empty `Observable`. If we change the previous example, using a function to test for odd numbers, we can see this behavior as follows:

```
Rx.Observable
    .of(2,4,5,6)
    .takeWhile((i)=>i%2===1)
    .subscribe((i)=>console.log(i));
```

If you run this code, you will see nothing printed in the console, as the first element (2) is not an odd number.

The skip() operator

The `skip()` operator returns an `Observable` which bypasses a given number of elements from the beginning and propagates the others until the completion of the `Observable`. It has the following signature:

```
observable.skip(count);
```

The only parameter is mandatory:

- `count`: This is the number of elements to bypass

In the following example, we will use the `skip()` operator to bypass the first element in the `Observable`:

```
Rx.Observable
    .of(1,2,3)
    .skip(1)
    .subscribe((i)=>console.log(i));
```

If you run this code, it will print the following:

2
3

This operation is illustrated in the following diagram:

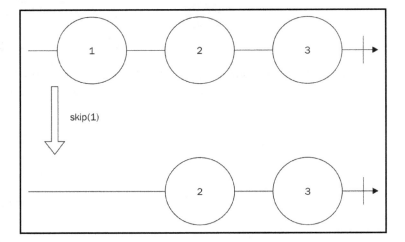

This operator can be used with the `take()` operator to extract a range from the original `Observable`:

```
Rx.Observable
    .of(1,2,3,4)
    .skip(1)
    .take(2)
    .subscribe((i)=>console.log(i));
```

In this example, we create an Observable from the values 1, 2, 3, and 4. We then skip the first, so now we have elements: 2 and 3. We finally take only two of them, so if we run this code, we will see the following output:

```
2
3
```

The skipWhile() operator

The last operator in this chapter, the skipWhile() operator, is analogous to the takeWhile() operator, but it skips the elements while a given conditional function is satisfied. It has the following signature:

```
observable.skipWhile(condition.[context]);
```

The first parameter is mandatory and the second is optional:

- condition: This is a function to test the elements to be skipped
- context: This is an argument to be used in the condition function

To illustrate this operator, we can use the same example from the takeWhile(), but using the skipWhile() function instead:

```
Rx.Observable
    .of(2,4,5,6)
    .skipWhile((i)=>i%2===0)
    .subscribe((i)=>console.log(i));
```

In this code, we will skip the even elements starting from the beginning of the sequence and stop when we find the first non-even number. So if we run this code, we will see the following output:

```
5
6
```

This operation is illustrated in the following diagram:

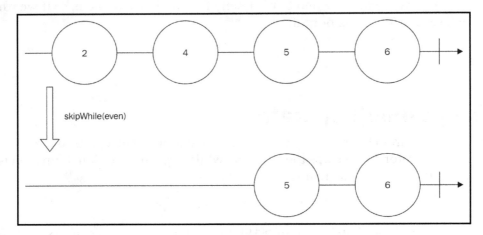

Summary

In this chapter, we learned how to deal with massive amounts of data. We called this the problem of backpressure. We can use two different approaches to deal with backpressure: lossy strategies and loss-less strategies.

We also learned about the advantages and disadvantages of each approach, and also which operators we can use to mitigate them.

At the end of the chapter, we also received more tools to query for data in our observables, such as the `first()` operator, some `take()` operators, and some `skip()` operators.

In the next chapter, we will learn about operators to combine different sources of data.

6
Too Many Sources - Combining Observables

In the last chapter, we learned how we can use different operators to deal with the backpressure problem, learned two different strategies to deal with this problem:

- Lossy strategy
- Loss-less strategy

For each strategy, we learned different operators implement a lossy strategy to deal with the back pressure problem. learned the following operators:

- `throttle()`
- `sample()`
- `debounce()`
- `pause()`

To implement a loss-less strategy to deal with the back pressure problem we learned the following operators:

- `bufferWithCount()`
- `bufferWithTime()`
- `bufferWithTimeOrCount()`
- `pause()` using buffering
- `controlled()`

We also learned when to use each strategy, based on the amount of memory we have available and if we can afford losing any data or not.

For the last, we learned new operators to filter data, along with the `filter()` operator. This operator lets us avoid computation of unnecessary events on an observable. We learned the following operators to filter data:

- `first()`
- `take()`
- `takeLast()`
- `takeWhile()`
- `skip()`
- `skipWhile()`

If you did not familiarize yourself with the problem of backpressure. Take time to read this chapter again, as this problem is very common and anyone calling themselves a master in functional reactive programming must be able to recognize and mitigate this problem.

In this chapter, we will see how we can combine different observables to create new observables, we will also use more complex and elaborate examples to teach the new concepts to get you out of your comfort zone and improve your functional reactive programming skills even more.

In this chapter, we will learn the following topics:

- When do I need to combine observables?
- Running observables in parallel
- Concatenating observables
- Combining data from different observables
- Reusing methods and operators from previous chapters in more complex examples

When do I need to combine observables?

One of the main advantages of functional reactive programming is how easy it makes reusing code, as we detach the source of data (observable) to the transformations we do on this data (operators) to the effect it causes when it happens (action taken by an observer), we can easily reuse each part of our code.

In the previous chapters, we saw how we can reuse an observable adding multiple observers to it. Now we can go one step further and combine these observables to create a new source of data; this will give us even more power.

When we combine (specifically when we concatenate) observables we can also avoid repeating code that is aligned with one of the main concepts of good code, which is **Don't Repeat Yourself** (DRY).

One simple and easy to understand example of combining observables to avoid subscribing to two observables can happen in a common task. Imagine that we want to implement a search tool in a website. On our search tool we want to do the search when the user hits *Enter* (and the search box has focus) or when the user clicks on the search button. Using RxJS it's easy to create an observable for clicks in the enter button for the search box using the `fromEvent()` method, and it's also easy to create an observable from clicks in the search button with the same method. Without the ability to concatenate both observables we would have to subscribe to each observable creating two different subscriptions. This is not only unnecessary, but it can also lead to errors as any subscription can be individually terminated. But as we will see in this chapter, we can concatenate both observables to create a new observable that emits data when any of the sources emits, and we will subscribe only to this observable to create code that is more readable, error prone, and semantically correct.

We also learned that we can use observables, to help us with the flow control of our application, using it to wrap promises or even callbacks. So we can also combine observables to run these asynchronous computations in parallel.

Running observables

Dealing with asynchronous computation in JavaScript is a hard task, and this is because all your code runs in a single thread. So, to keep this thread available most operators dealing with I/O use a callback to return the control to your program when the data is available.

 The concept of threads and how JavaScript virtual machines work internally goes beyond the scope of this book, and it is not necessary to understand it.

The extensive use of callback functions usually leads to a problem called **callback hell**, which is basically a code with too many callbacks making it really hard to read from a programmer perspective. To mitigate this problem, promises are now part of the standard JavaScript and are implemented by all modern browsers. As promises are composable by nature, it makes your code cleaner and gives you a safe way out from callback hell.

But promises have only basic constructs to compose with each other, and for this reason RxJS (and most functional reactive programming libraries in JavaScript) gives you built-in methods to turn a promise in an observable making it even more composable with the usage of operators.

With that said, it is easy to see why functional reactive programming, with the power of concatenating and combining observables (which can be asynchronous computation), is a natural solution to deal with your application flow control.

Concatenating observables

RxJS enables some operators to combine several observables in a single one containing the events from all, the most common operators are `concat()` and `merge()`, which simply creates a new observable containing all data from the others, but in this chapter we will also learn how to do more interesting combinations with other operators.

Using the concat() operator

The most common operator to concatenate two sources of data (observables) is the `concat()` operator. This operator receives multiple observables as arguments and concatenates all observables from the left to right. It preserves the order of the elements in the observables and only propagates data from the next observable if the current one is already terminated.

This operator has the following signature:

```
observable.concat(observables);
```

It accepts any number of arguments, but they all must be observables:

* `observable`: It is any number of observables

The easiest possible example is to use it to combine two observables:

```
Rx.Observable
    .just(1)
    .concat(Rx.Observable.just(2))
    .subscribe((k)=>console.log(k));
```

In this code we create an `Observable` sequence that contains only the element 1. We then use the `concat()` operator to concatenate it with an `Observable` sequence, which contains only the element 2, and we finally `subscribe` to `log` all elements in the final `Observable`. So if we run this code we will see the following output:

```
1
2
```

This code can be explained by the following diagram:

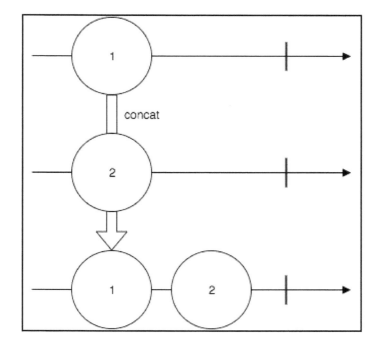

Now let's slightly change our code to concatenate another `Observable`:

```
Rx.Observable
  .just(1)
  .concat(
    Rx.Observable.just(2),
    Rx.Observable.just('Hello World!!!')
  ).subscribe((k)=>console.log(k));
```

As we only added another observable that emits the value 3, it is easy to understand the output of this program, as follows:

```
1
2
Hello World!!!
```

This implementation is possible because the `concat()` operator accepts multiple observables as parameters, but the same program can also be written as follows:

```
Rx.Observable
  .just(1)
  .concat(Rx.Observable.just(2))
  .concat(Rx.Observable.just('Hello World!!!'))
  .subscribe((k)=>console.log(k));
```

If we use the `concat()` operator twice instead of calling it with two parameters, the result is the same.

As we discussed before, the `concat()` operator keeps the order of the input when generating the new `Observable`, and only emits data from the next `Observable` when the current finishes. We can see this behavior doing a minor change on our example, as follows:

```
Rx.Observable
  .just(1)
  .concat(
    Rx.Observable.interval(1000),
    Rx.Observable.just('Hello World!!!')
  ).subscribe((k)=>console.log(k));
```

In this example, the final `Observable` will emit the value of the first one (value 1), and as it finishes it goes to the next. As the `Observable` created from the `interval()` method is infinite, it will never emit the `Hello World!!!` string from the last `Observable`. So running this code will give us the following output, and it keeps printing consecutive numbers until we kill the program:

```
1
0
1
2
3
//Keeps printing until we stop the program
```

Using the merge() operator

In the last section, we learned to use the `concat()` operator to concatenate observables keeping the order of each observable from left to right. We also saw that if one of the observables is infinite, the other observables after this will never propagate this data. When we want to concatenate observables preserving the order of the data instead of the order of the observable, we use the `merge()` operator.

This operator has the following signature:

```
observable.merge(observable);
```

It accepts any number of arguments, but they all must be observables:

- `observable`: This is the other observable to be merged

 There is another signature for this method where you can set the maximum number of observables being subscribed to concurrently, but this is uncommon to use in RxJS and we will avoid it in this book, to make the concept easier to understand.

We can change the first example of the `concat()` operator and use the `merge()` operator to combine two observables:

```
Rx.Observable
  .just(1)
  .merge(Rx.Observable.just(2))
  .subscribe((k)=>console.log(k));
```

In this example, we just changed the `concat()` operator for the `merge()` operator, but as we have no infinite observable nor an asynchronous one, we can't see any difference on the output, as follows:

```
1
2
```

Now let's change the previous example, which uses an `Observable` created with the `interval()` method:

```
Rx.Observable
  .just(1)
  .merge(Rx.Observable.interval(1000))
  .merge(Rx.Observable.just('Hello World!!!'))
  .subscribe((k)=>console.log(k));
```

In the previous session we saw the output from a code like this, but using `concat()` instead of `merge()`, and in that example the `Hello World!!!` message doesn't get printed because the `Observable` created from `interval()` never finishes and as the `concat()` operator preserves the order of the observables, it never propagates data from the last. But the `merge()` operator preserves the order when the data is propagated and for this reason when we run this code we see this output in the console:

```
1
Hello World!!!
0
1
2
//Keeps printing sequential numbers until we stops the program
```

This code can be explained by the following diagram:

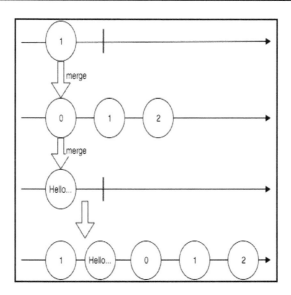

Previously in this chapter we showed an example usage of observables concatenation to create a search box (or any textbox), which takes an action when the user hits the Enter button or when it clicks on a related button. The `merge()` operator is perfect for implementing this behavior in a web page, and this can be seen in the following example:

```
<html>
  <head></head>
  <body>

    <input type="text" id="my_input"/>
    <button id="my_button">Search</button>
    <span id="my_span"></span>

    <script
src="https://cdnjs.cloudflare.com/ajax/libs/rxjs/4.1.0/rx.all.js"></script>
    <script>
      var enterKeyUpObservable = Rx.Observable
        .fromEvent(document.getElementById("my_input"),"keyup")
        .filter(function(e){
          return e.keyCode===13;
        });

      var searchClickObservable = Rx.Observable
        .fromEvent(document.getElementById("my_button"),"click");

      var enterKeyUpOrSearchClickObservable =
searchClickObservable.merge(enterKeyUpObservable);
```

```
        enterKeyUpOrSearchClickObservable.subscribe(function(){
          var text = document.getElementById("my_input").value;
          document.getElementById('my_span').innerHTML = "searched for ===>
"+text;
        });
    </script>
  </body>
</html>
```

In this code we create an `Observable` from all Enter key up events (`var enterKeyUpObservable`), then we create an `Observable` from all clicks in the search button (`var searchClickObservable`). We finally merge both observables using the `merge()` operator, which gives us a new `Observable`, (`var enterKeyUpOrSearchClickObservable`) and subscribe to it to fill a span element with a message.

 To implement this behavior we must use the `merge()` operator. If we tried to use the `concat()` operator instead, it would listen only for the left most observable, as it is an infinite observable. If you are curious, change this code to use the `concat()` operator instead of the `merge()` operator and test the page.

If you open it in your browser you will see the following screen:

You can test this page by typing any content in the textbox and executing the subscription function by hitting *Enter* in the textbox or clicking on the **Search** button.

Using the concatAll() operator

This operator is analogous to the `concat()` operator, but it concatenates all observables inside an `observable`. This operator has the following signature:

```
observable.concatAll();
```

As you can see, it does not receive any parameter as it will concatenate all `observable` within an `observable`. This behavior can be seen in the following example:

```
Rx.Observable.of(
  Rx.Observable.just(1),
  Rx.Observable.fromPromise(Promise.resolve(2)),
  Rx.Observable.of(3,4)
).concatAll()
.subscribe((k)=>console.log(k));
```

In this example, we create an `Observable` using the `of()` method, containing three observables. The first only emits the value `1`, the second only emits the value `2` (using a `Promise`), and the third emits two values `3` and `4`. We then use the method `concatAll()` to generate a single `Observable` that emits four values. So, if we run this code we will see the following output in your console:

```
1
2
3
4
```

> This method follows the same rules from the `concat()` method, so it will follow the observables order and if you have an infinite `observable` in your sequence, the next `observable` will never be executed.

Using the mergeAll() operator

This method is analogous to the `concatAll()` operator following the `merge()` operator rules. So it merges all observables within an `observable`. It has the following signature:

```
observable.mergeAll();
```

As you can see, it does not receive any parameter as it will merge all observables within an `observable`. This behavior can be seen in the following example:

```
Rx.Observable.of(
  Rx.Observable.just(1),
  Rx.Observable.fromPromise(Promise.resolve(2)),
  Rx.Observable.of(3,4)
).mergeAll()
.subscribe((k)=>console.log(k));
```

Now that we are using the `mergeAll()` operator instead of the `concatAll()` operator, it will follow the order of the propagated data, and as we have an `Observable` from a `Promise`, its value will be delayed (because the promise is asynchronous) and the other values will be propagated first, so it will print the following output in your console:

```
1
3
4
2
```

Combining observables

We already learned how we can create an observable containing all data from the other observables, but we can also use some other operators to combine this data or choose between them instead of just propagating everything.

Using the forkJoin() operator

This operator lets you run multiple observables in parallel and propagates the last elements of each one, so this operator is perfect for implementing flow control for promises or callback operations in JavaScript, as we already discussed in this chapter.

This operator has the following signature:

```
Rx.Observable.forkJoin(observables);
```

This is a `class()` method instead of an `instance()` method, and it receives an arbitrary number of arguments and the last is optional:

- `observables`: An arbitrary number of observable sequences to be executed

 It can also accept a last argument to concatenate the items of the produced array, but this is not a common use case as you can easily do it using the `map()` operator over the array.

The `forkJoin()` operator preserves the order of the observables and an example of this usage can be seen in the following code:

```
Rx.Observable
  .forkJoin(
    Rx.Observable.fromPromise(Promise.resolve(1)),
    Rx.Observable.just(2)
  ).subscribe((k)=>console.log(k));
```

If you run this code, you will see the following output:

```
[ 1, 2 ]
```

As we discussed previously, this operator propagates only the last value of each observable sequence, which makes it perfect for promises and callbacks (which emit only one value), but we can use it with any `Observable`.

We can change our code to use an infinite `Observable` and see what happens:

```
Rx.Observable
  .forkJoin(
    Rx.Observable.fromPromise(Promise.resolve(1)),
    Rx.Observable.interval(100)
  ).subscribe((k)=>console.log(k));
```

If you run this code, you will see nothing printed in the console and your program also never ends. This happens because the second parameter is an infinite observable, so the `forkJoin()` operator will wait for it to finish to propagate all values.

We can change this code to take only a few elements from the infinite `Observable`. This way it will finish:

```
Rx.Observable
  .forkJoin(
    Rx.Observable.fromPromise(Promise.resolve(1)),
    Rx.Observable.interval(100).take(5)
  ).subscribe((k)=>console.log(k));
```

Now if you run this code, you will see the following output:

```
[ 1, 4 ]
```

This contains the value 1 propagated by the first `Observable` and the value 4, which is the last element (as we took 5 from the `interval()`) propagated by the second `Observable`.

This operation can be described by the following diagram:

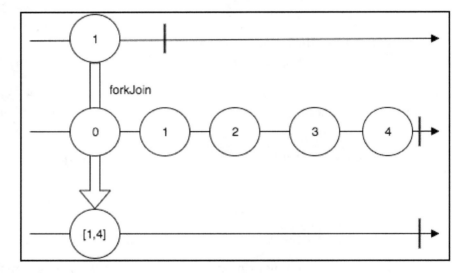

Using the zip() operator

This operator lets you merge the values of given observables. It will run a given function for each element of each observable of the same index. So if you have two observables and you zip them, it will run your given function for the first element of the first observable and the first element of the second observable. If more elements are available, it will run the function for the second element of the first observable, the second element of the second observable, and so on.

 This operator is analogous to the `zip()` function of libraries such as `underscore` and `lodash`.

This operator has the following signature:

```
Rx.Observable.zip(observables, [reduceFunction]);
```

It receives an arbitrary number of arguments, and the last is optional. In case of absence of the last parameter, it will only generate an array with the values of each `observable`:

- `observables`: This is any number of `observables` to be zipped
- `reduceFunction`: This is a function used to combine the elements in a single value; if this function is not provided, it will generate an array with the values

A simple example of `zip()` operator usage would be zipping two observables, each one containing two values omitting the `reduceFunction` parameter, like you can see in the following code:

```
var namesObservable = Rx.Observable.of('John', 'Mary');

var lastNamesObservable = Rx.Observable.of('Doe', 'Jane');

Rx.Observable.zip(
    namesObservable,
    lastNamesObservable
).subscribe((k)=>console.log(k));
```

If you run this code you will see the following output in your console:

```
[ 'John', 'Doe' ]
[ 'Mary', 'Jane' ]
```

This code can be described by this diagram:

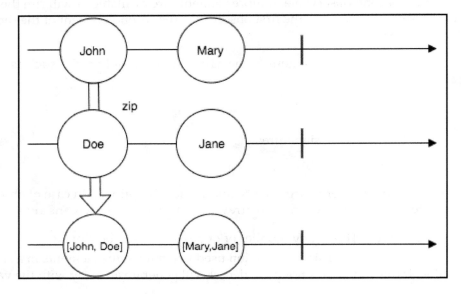

We can pass `reduceFunction` to make the output more interesting:

```
var namesObservable = Rx.Observable.of('John', 'Mary');

var lastNamesObservable = Rx.Observable.of('Doe', 'Jane');

Rx.Observable.zip(
    namesObservable,
    lastNamesObservable,
    (name,lastName) => name + ' ' + lastName
).subscribe((k)=>console.log(k));
```

In this example, the given function will be executed for each pair, as the function basically concatenates `name` and `lastName`. The `Observable` generated by the `zip()` operator in this example contains the full name of `John` and `Mary`, so when we `subscribe()` to it and `log` the result to the console we can see output as follows:

```
John Doe
Mary Jane
```

This operator can also be called for more observables. In the following example we will zip three Observables:

```
Rx.Observable
  .zip(
    Rx.Observable.just(1),
    Rx.Observable.fromPromise(Promise.resolve(2)),
    Rx.Observable.just(3)
  ).subscribe((k)=>console.log(k));
```

When you run this code, you can see the following output:

```
[ 1, 2, 3 ]
```

Looking at the output from this last example is easy to see that the `zip()` operator gives the results using the same order from the observables waiting for each element of the current iteration to be available before propagating it.

Now you might be wondering what happens when one of the `Observable` finishes before the others. Let's check this in the following example:

```
Rx.Observable
  .zip(
    Rx.Observable.interval(100),
    Rx.Observable.just('second'),
    Rx.Observable.of('third', 'more on third observable')
  ).subscribe((k)=>console.log(k));
```

When we run this code we see the following output in the console and the program exits:

```
[ 0, 'second', 'third' ]
```

Looking at the output, it is easy to see that the `Observable` generated by the `zip()` operator finishes when the first `Observable` being zipped finishes.

Using the zipIterable() operator

The `zipIterable()` operator works similarly to the `zip()` operator. The only difference is it lets you zip observables with JavaScript `iterables` objects such as arrays, sets, and maps.

This operator has the following signature:

```
observable.zipIterable(iterables, [reduceFunction]);
```

It receives an arbitrary number of arguments, and the last is optional. In case of absence of the last parameter, it will only generate an array with the values:

- `iterables`: This is any number of `iterables` to be zipped with the observable
- `reduceFunction`: This is a function used to combine the elements in a single value; if this function is not provided, it will generate an array with the values

We can do a minor change in our first example using the `zip()` operator to use the `zipIterable()` operator over an `iterables` object:

```
var namesObservable = Rx.Observable.of('John', 'Mary');

var lastNamesArray = ['Doe', 'Jane'];

namesObservable
  .zipIterable(lastNamesArray)
  .subscribe((k)=>console.log(k));
```

If you run this code, you will see an output as follows:

```
[ 'John', 'Doe' ]
[ 'Mary', 'Jane' ]
```

We can also change it to use a `reduceFunction`, as we did with the `zip()` operator:

```
var namesObservable = Rx.Observable.of('John', 'Mary');

var lastNamesArray = ['Doe', 'Jane'];

namesObservable
  .zipIterable(
    lastNamesArray,
    (name,lastName) => name + ' ' + lastName
  ).subscribe((k)=>console.log(k));
```

As we expect, the output is as follows:

```
John Doe
Mary Jane
```

And for the last, we can use the same code with other forms of iterables such as `Set()`:

```
var namesObservable = Rx.Observable.of('John', 'Mary');

var lastNamesArray = new Set(['Doe', 'Jane']);

namesObservable
  .zipIterable(
    lastNamesArray,
    (name,lastName) => name + ' ' + lastName
  ).subscribe((k)=>console.log(k));
```

 The `zipIterable()` operator is similar to the `zip()` operator. It only makes it easier to interoperate observables and regular iterables.

Summary

In this chapter, we focused on the benefits of combining observables; we learned that we can use them to run asynchronous tasks in parallel, avoid code repetition when listening to multiple sources, and improve code reuse and readability.

We also learned different operators to combine and unify observables. The most common and most used observables for doing so are `concat()`, `merge()`, and `zip()`.

But we also learned about some other operators to combine observables as they give us more tools to interoperate our code.

Upto now we have just ignored possible errors propagated by an observable. In the next chapter, the focus will be handling these errors and creating tests for our functional reactive applications. So, we will learn detecting errors in observables, handling errors in observables, mocking observables, and testing functional reactive programs.

7
Something is Wrong - Testing and Dealing with Errors

In the last chapter we learned about a powerful tool to increase the reuse and readability of our code. This tool is a combination of observables to create new sources of data. We also learned how we can run multiple asynchronous observables in parallel.

The most important operators we learned in the previous chapter are:

- `concat()`
- `merge()`
- `forkJoin()`
- `zip()`

The use of this operators can help us to avoid code repetition, giving us one very important mantra for readable code: **Don't Repeat Yourself** (**DRY**).

In this chapter, we will focus on two very important issues, not only for programs implemented using functional reactive programming, but for all programs:

- Dealing with errors
- Testing our code
    - We will see what happens to an observable when an error occurs and what we can do to treat this error and ensure our code keeps running as expected.

- On the other hand, one of the coolest things about functional reactive programming is the ability to decouple the source of your data from the action to be executed This makes our code more testable, as we can mock any part of it.
- In this chapter we will learn how to test programs on the browser and in Node.js. For those without any familiarity with testing JavaScript code, we will have a quick look at some frameworks for doing so.
- As we advance in this book the main idea is to make our examples more complex. We will see this development in the test section, so take time to review the previous chapters now, or anytime you see an operator you are not familiar with yet.

Dealing with errors

Detecting and treating errors in asynchronous code are hard tasks. For synchronous code, we can use the famous `try/catch/finally` block. Treating an exception with this block is easy, as can be seen in the following code:

```
try{
  throw new Error('An error occurred');
}catch(err){
  console.log('Treating the error');
}finally{
  console.log('Last computation');
}
```

Unfortunately, we can't use the `try/catch/finally` on asynchronous code. In JavaScript we run asynchronous code most of the time, so the language and the community elaborated a couple of strategies.

Initially, the only strategy we had available to deal with asynchronous code was the use of callback functions, so most libraries in JavaScript added the `onSuccess()` and `onError()` methods, which accepted a callback function to be executed when an error happened or when data is available. Different frameworks used different methods for doing so, for example, in jQuery it was `ajaxError()` and `ajaxSuccess()`. The Node.js community saw the necessity for standardizing this behavior (as this is really common in JavaScript), and so the Node.js callback standard was created.

This standard enforces the use of a single function, which receives two parameters for asynchronous computation: the first is an error object (if an error happened) and the second is the successful result (if it was a success). The callback standard from node can still be seen in the core functions and in several libraries. An example of this standard is available in the `fs` module, which is the module from node that interacts with the file system:

```
var fs = require('fs');

fs.readFile('this_file_doesnt_exist.txt', function(e, data) {
   if(e) {
     console.log('An error happened');
     return;
   }
   console.log(data);
});
```

> If you have any prior experience with Node.js you are already be familiar with this pattern.

As you probably know, using callbacks can lead to a problem called callback hell, which happens when you have several callbacks running inside each other, and which makes your code hard to understand. So, the `Promise` object was created and this includes a `catch()` method to treat errors:

```
new Promise(function(resolve, reject) {
   reject(new Error('An error occurred'));
}).catch(function(err) {
   console.log('Treating the error');
});
```

In this code we have a failed `Promise` where the error is treated using the `catch()` method. As you can see, none of these options are as easy as the standard `try/catch/finally`, but such a solution is not yet available for asynchronous code, so we have to use one of the available strategies.

> In upcoming versions of JavaScript, we will have the async/await feature, which will let us use the `try/catch/finally` block again.

In functional reactive programming, we have different strategies to deal with errors, which we will see in this section.

Acting when an error occurs

When an error occurs, the observable stops sending new data. We can use different strategies, such as switching to another observable or retry, but these are more advanced so first we will see how an observer can be notified by an error. As you probably remember, the subscribe() method from the observable object lets you pass up to three functions or allows an observer to be notified when an error occurs.

Take a look at the following signature:

```
observable.subscribe([onNext], [onError], [onCompleted]);
```

The parameters are optional:

- onNext: This function is to be called when new data is available in this observable. The function receives the data itself as a parameter.
- onError: This function is to be called when an error is propagated through this observable. This function received the Error as a parameter.
- onCompleted: This function is to be called when the observable is exhausted and all the data has already been propagated.

This method also has an overloaded implementation with the following signature:

```
observable.subscribe(observer);
```

It accepts this single parameter:

- observer: The observer object is to be notified when some data is available, an error happens, or the observable is exhausted. The observer has specific methods for each of these possible events.

So, we have two possible ways to be notified of an error in an `observable`; the first is as follows:

```
Rx.Observable
  .throw(new Error('An error occurred'))
  .subscribe(
  (data)=> console.log(data),
  (e)=> console.log('ERROR'),
  ()=>console.log('finished')
);
```

The second, is an implementation explicitly using an `observer` object:

```
var observer = Rx.Observer
  .create(
  (data)=> console.log(data),
  (e)=> console.log('ERROR'),
  ()=>console.log('finished')
);
Rx.Observable
  .throw(new Error('An error occurred'))
  .subscribe(observer);
```

The two implementations are equivalent, and if you run either of these codes, you will see the following output:

ERROR

As you can see the `onCompleted()` function is not called when an error is propagated to the observer.

As we have already discussed, when an error occurs the `observable` stops. We can see this behavior in the following code:

```
var observable = Rx.Observable.create(function(source){
  source.onNext(1);

  source.onError(new Error('An error occurred'));

  source.onNext(2);
  source.onCompleted();
});

observable.subscribe(
  (data)=> console.log(data),
  (e)=> console.log('ERROR'),
  ()=>console.log('finished')
);
```

In this code, we create an `observable` that will call first the `onNext()` with the 1, then the `onError()` with an `Error` object, then again the `onNext()` with 2, and finally the `onCompleted()` method. If you run this code, you will see the following output:

```
1
ERROR
```

As we expected, it stopped propagating any data or event after the error. This is the default behavior but sometimes we might need other tools to treat our errors before it gets to the observer, and we will see these strategies in the next section.

Treating an error

In the last section, we learned to react to errors on our observer, but we have other strategies to deal with errors before propagating them to our observers. These strategies include the following points:

- Fallback to a different observable
- Retry the computation of this observable
- Delay the delivery of the error

These strategies can be implemented using operators that we will explore in the chapter.

The catch() operator

The `catch()` operator lets you try another observable. When an error occurs it can be used at the class or instance level.

At the class level, the `catch()` operator has the following signature:

```
Rx.Observable.catch(observables);
```

As you can see, it receives an arbitrary number of arguments:

- `observables`: It is an arbitrary number of observables to be used as fallback in the first failure. They are attempted from left to right until an `Observable` succeeds.

The simplest way to see this operator in action is with the following example:

```
Rx.Observable.catch(
    Rx.Observable.throw(new Error('An error occurred')),
    Rx.Observable.just('Hello')
).subscribe(
  (m) => console.log(m),
  (e) => console.log('Error found')
);
```

In this example, we call `catch()` from the `Observable` class, so it will try the first `Observable`. As this `Observable` fails (it was created using `throw()`), it will try the next one, which succeeds. Then this `Observable` is propagated, notifying the observer of the data, so when you run this code you will see the `Hello` message printed in your console.

Now, let's see what happens if the first `observable` emits some data, before propagating any error:

```
var observableWithError = Rx.Observable.create(function(source){
    source.onNext(1);

    source.onError(new Error('An error occurred'));

    source.onNext(2);
    source.onCompleted();
});

Rx.Observable.catch(
  observableWithError,
  Rx.Observable.just('Hello')
).subscribe(
  (m) => console.log(m),
  (e) => console.log('Error found')
);
```

If you run this code you will see the following output:

```
1
Hello
```

So, it will propagate all the data before the error to the observer and, when the error happens, it will go to the next `Observable`.

Now let's see what happens if the second `Observable` also fails, but we have a third `Observable`:

```
Rx.Observable.catch(
  Rx.Observable.throw(new Error('An error occurred')),
  Rx.Observable.throw(new Error('Another error occurred')),
  Rx.Observable.just('Hello')
).subscribe(
  (m)=> console.log(m),
  (e)=> console.log('Error found')
);
```

In this case, it will attempt the first `Observable`, but as it fails it will attempt the second `Observable`. As this also fails, it will attempt the third observable, which succeeds. If you run this code you will see the `Hello` message printed in your console.

For the last example, let's see what happens when the first `Observable` succeeds:

```
Rx.Observable.catch(
  Rx.Observable.just('Hello'),
  Rx.Observable.just('Hello again')
).subscribe(
  (m)=> console.log(m),
  (e)=> console.log('Error found')
);
```

The `catch()` operator works exactly like the `try/catch` block, so if the attempted observable runs without any error, it will never pass the execution for the following. This way, when you run this code you see the following output in your console:

Hello

The `catch()` operator when used in an instance of an `Observable` works the same way, using that `Observable` as the first attempt, but it only accepts one parameter, as you can see in the following example:

```
Rx.Observable
  .throw(new Error('An error occurred'))
  .catch(Rx.Observable.just('Hello'))
  .subscribe(
    (m)=> console.log(m),
    (e)=> console.log('Error found')
  );
```

This code works exactly like the previous one; as you expected, it will print the `Hello` message in your console.

If you want multiple `catch()` in an `Observable` instance, you will have to call the `catch()` operator multiple times:

```
Rx.Observable
  .throw(new Error('An error occurred'))
  .catch(Rx.Observable.throw(new Error('Another error occurred')))
  .catch(Rx.Observable.just('Hello'))
  .subscribe(
    (m)=> console.log(m),
    (e)=> console.log('Error found')
  );
```

The onErrorResumeNext() operator

The operator `onErrorResumeNext()` runs a list of observables from left to right, passing to the next observable either when the current observable finishes, or when an error occurs. This method is available in the `Observable` class and has the following signature:

```
Rx.Observable.onErrorResumeNext(observables);
```

As you can see it receives an arbitrary number of arguments:

- `observables`: It is an arbitrary number of observables to be executed from left to right; the next observable starts when the current finishes or fails.

We can use some of the examples from the previous section, changing only the operator to illustrate how the `onErrorResumeNext()` operator works:

```
Rx.Observable.onErrorResumeNext(
  Rx.Observable.throw(new Error('An error occurred')),
  Rx.Observable.just('Hello')
).subscribe(
  (m)=> console.log(m),
  (e)=> console.log('Error found')
);
```

In this code, the `onErrorResumeNext()` operator will create an `Observable` that executes the first `Observable` and the second when the first fails; thus, when you run this code you will see the `Hello` message printed in your console. However, with this example we can not really distinguish it from the `catch()` operator, so let's try a different example: we'll create three `Observable`, one of these `Observables` will propagate a value and then fail, and the other two will propagate a value each and completes with success. All three `Observable` can be seen in the following code:

```
var observableWithError = Rx.Observable.create(function(source){
    source.onNext(1);

    source.onError(new Error('An error occurred'));

    source.onNext(2);
    source.onCompleted();
});
var helloObservable = Rx.Observable.just('Hello');
var helloAgainObservable = Rx.Observable.just('Hello again');
```

Now, in the same program, let's use the `onErrorResumeNext()` operator and the `catch()` operator with the three `Observable` to compare the output:

```
Rx.Observable.onErrorResumeNext(
    observableWithError,
    helloObservable,
    helloAgainObservable
).subscribe(
    (m)=> console.log('onErrorResumeNext operator propagated ===> ' + m),
    (e)=> console.log('Error found')
);

Rx.Observable.catch(
    observableWithError,
    helloObservable,
    helloAgainObservable
).subscribe(
    (m)=> console.log('catch operator propagated===> '+m),
    (e)=> console.log('Error found')
);
```

The use of these operators in this example is simple. We only call each operator for the three observables and `subscribe()` to listen to data (or an error) in each of them so that we can compare the outputs. When you execute this program, you will see the following output in your console:

```
onErrorResumeNext operator propagated ===> 1
onErrorResumeNext operator propagated ===> Hello
onErrorResumeNext operator propagated ===> Hello again
catch operator propagated===> 1
catch operator propagated===> Hello
```

Looking at this output it's easy to see that the `catch()` operator has the same behavior as the `try/catch` block from synchronous computation, while the `onErrorResumeNext()` attempts to execute all observables.

 The `catch()` operator tries an observable and handles the execution to the next only when it fails, while the `onErrorResumeNext()` executes all observables from left to right, passing to the next when the current one completes or fails.

The retry() operator

This operator again lets you execute an `observable` a given number of times in the presence of an error. The most common use case is to do an HTTP call to a resource and retry a couple of times if an error happens. The `retry()` operator has the following signature:

```
observable.retry(retryAttempts);
```

It receives only one parameter:

- `retryAttempts`: This is a number indicating the number of times this `observable` must be retried.

To test this operator we will try to fetch the Google search page and retry it three times before propagating the error (you can change the Google page for any other URL). To do so, we will use the `request-promise` library, which fetches a URL using `promise()`, and then use the `fromPromise()` method to create an `Observable` from that `promise()`. First, we need to install the `request-promise` and the `request` library for node:

```
npm i request@2.79.0 --save
npm i request-promise@4.1.1 --save
```

Then we can use the following code to implement the described behavior:

```
var Rx = require('rx');
var request = require('request-promise');

Rx.Observable.fromPromise(
   request('http://www.google.com')
).retry(3)
.subscribe(
   (htmlPage)=>console.log(htmlPage)
);
```

If you execute this code you will see the Google page printed in your console.

You can try this operator for any intermittent resource you have available to see exactly how it works.

The mergeDelayError() operator

The last operator that deals with errors in this chapter is the `mergeDelayError()` operator. When you merge two or more observables (using the `merge()` operator), if an error is propagated from one of the observables, it will be propagated to the generated observable stopping it, as you can see in the following example:

```
var observableWithError = Rx.Observable.create(function(source){
   source.onNext('hello');

   source.onError(new Error('An error occurred'));

   source.onNext('hello again');
   source.onCompleted();
});

Rx.Observable.merge(
   observableWithError,
   Rx.Observable.interval(100).take(4)
).subscribe(
   (m)=>console.log(m),
   (e)=>console.log('Error')
);
```

In this example, we create an `Observable` that emits a value (1) and then an error. We use the `merge()` operator to merge it with an `Observable` generated from an `interval()` (where we take only four values). When you execute this you will see the following output:

```
hello
Error
```

Looking at the output we can see that the generated `Observable` only propagated the first element from the first `Observable`. It didn't have the chance to propagate the `Observable` created from the `interval()`.

Now, let's change this code to use the `mergeDelayError()` operator instead:

```
var observableWithError = Rx.Observable.create(function(source){
    source.onNext('hello');

    source.onError(new Error('An error occurred'));

    source.onNext('hello again');
    source.onCompleted();
});

Rx.Observable.mergeDelayError(
    observableWithError,
    Rx.Observable.interval(100).take(4)
).subscribe(
    (m)=>console.log(m),
    (e)=>console.log('Error')
);
```

If you run this code you will see the following output:

```
hello
0
1
2
3
Error
```

Now the output has changed; the use of the `mergeDelayError()` was delayed (until all the other observables had finished) to propagate the error.

The `mergeDelayError()` has the following signature:

```
Rx.Observable.mergeDelayError(...observables);
```

It accepts any number of arguments, but they all must be `observables`:

- `observables`: It is the `observables` to be merged

This is enough information for now on how to deal with errors in RxJS.

Testing our application

Testing an application is one of the main concerns for programmers. It does not matter what paradigms, languages, or frameworks you are using to develop your program, you must always be careful with your tests.

A good test suite ensures better quality for your code and for your application. It can also be used by other programmers to help them read and understand your code, and it helps you decouple and improve the architecture for your program.

This book is not about tests, so I will not try to evangelize them but I advise you to always test your code, and it's vital. I will give you some advice and show how functional reactive programming can help you to decouple your code, increasing its testability.

Before jumping in to any explanation or code, let's learn the basics of unit testing in JavaScript. If you already test your JavaScript code, you can jump to the *Testing applications using RxJS* section.

Testing in the server

The first thing you need when testing JavaScript applications is a test-runner.

The test-runner is the program that gives you the tools to create your tests, executes them, and provide the test results. One very famous `test-runner` for Node.js is called `mocha`, and this is the runner we will be using in this book when doing tests on the server.

First, we need to install it using the following command:

```
npm install mocha@3.2.0 —save-dev
```

Now let's create a basic test to see how it works:

```
var assert = require('assert');
describe('Math test', function() {
  it('should return -1 when evaluating the minimum between -1 and 1',
function() {
    assert.equal(-1, Math.min(-1,1));
  });
  it('should return 1 when evaluating the maximum between -1 and 1',
function() {
    assert.equal(1, Math.max(-1,1));
  });
});
```

In this code we required the assert module to do the assertions of our test. The `describe()` function lets you group several tests under a given title, and the `it()` function executes a given test function. So, here we create a group called `Math test` to test mathematical functions from the JavaScript `Math` class. In this group, we have two tests, which are the functions passed as arguments to the `it()` function; the first is a test for the `Math.min()` function and the other is a test for the `Math.max()` function.

To run this test, you have to execute the following command in your terminal:

mocha example_mocha_test_7_18.js

Here, `example_mocha_test_7_18.js` is the name of the file containing my example; if you execute this test you will see the following content in your console:

```
[bash-3.2$ mocha example_mocha_test_7_18.js


  Math test
    ✓ should return -1 when evaluating the minimum between -1 and 1
    ✓ should return 1 when evaluating the maximum between -1 and 1


  2 passing (7ms)
```

This output shows we executed two tests under the `Math test` group and both succeeded.

Now let's change the second test to make it fail:

```
var assert = require('assert');
describe('Math test', function() {
  it('should return -1 when evaluating the minimum between -1 and 1',
```

```
  function() {
    assert.equal(0, Math.min(-1,1));
  });
  it('should return 1 when evaluating the maximum between -1 and 1',
  function() {
    assert.equal(1, Math.max(-1,1));
  });
});
```

The only change was made in the assertion of the second test. Now our test will expect 0 to be the minimum between -1 and 1 (notice the test is wrong and is being used only to illustrate what happens when a test fails). Now run your test again, and you will see the following output:

```
Math test
  1) should return -1 when evaluating the minimum between -1 and 1
  ✓ should return 1 when evaluating the maximum between -1 and 1


1 passing (12ms)
1 failing

1) Math test should return -1 when evaluating the minimum between -1 and 1:

    AssertionError: 0 == -1
    + expected - actual

    -0
    +-1

    at Context.<anonymous> (example_mocha_test_7_19.js:4:12)
```

Now it shows that one test passed and one test failed. For the failure, it also shows the expected value, the received value, and the line where it occurred, which of course makes it easier to find your error (in this case it's an error in our test) to fix it.

 The mocha is the runner we will be using to test all server codes in this book.

Testing in the browser

In the last section we learned how to use `mocha` in a Node.js environment, but this framework can also be used to execute client-side tests in a browser environment. To do this we need to create an HTML page and add the CSS and `js` of `mocha` to it:

To add the `mocha.css` you add the following line in your HTML:

```
<link href="https://cdn.rawgit.com/mochajs/mocha/2.2.5/mocha.css"
rel="stylesheet" />
```

To add the JavaScript you add the following line in your HTML:

```
<script src="https://cdn.rawgit.com/mochajs/mocha/2.2.5/mocha.js"></script>
```

On the server side we could use the default assert module from Node.js, but as this module is not available in the browser context, we will have to add a library to handle the assertions of our code. The library we will use is called `chai`. To add it to your HTML page just add the following line:

```
<script
src="https://cdnjs.cloudflare.com/ajax/libs/chai/3.5.0/chai.min.js"></scrip
t>
```

Now you are ready to execute your tests inside the browser context. The same example tests for the `Math` class we saw in the last section are implemented in this HTML file:

```
<html>
  <head>
    <meta charset="utf-8">
    <title>Tests</title>
    <link href="https://cdn.rawgit.com/mochajs/mocha/2.2.5/mocha.css"
rel="stylesheet" />
  </head>
  <body>
    <div id="mocha"></div>

    <script
src="https://cdn.rawgit.com/mochajs/mocha/2.2.5/mocha.js"></script>
    <script
src="https://cdnjs.cloudflare.com/ajax/libs/chai/3.5.0/chai.min.js"></scrip
t>
    <script>
      mocha.setup('bdd');
      var assert = chai.assert;
      describe('Math test', function() {
        it('should return -1 when evaluating the minimum between -1 and 1',
```

```
function() {
        assert.equal(-1, Math.min(-1,1));
      });
      it('should return 1 when evaluating the maximum between -1 and 1',
function() {
        assert.equal(1, Math.max(-1,1));
      });
    });
    mocha.run();
  </script>
</body>
</html>
```

Just some additional notes in this HTML file:

- Mocha also needs a `<div>` with `id` mocha to render the test results.
- You need to call `mocha.setup` before your tests; in our case `mocha.setup('bdd')` exposes the `describe()` and `it()` functions used in our tests.
- Your tests are executed when you call `mocha.run()`, so ensure you call it after your test code.

If you open this HTML page in your browser you will see a page like the following screenshot:

Running you code in the browser lets you access DOM elements in your code and in your tests, and we can create a simple test to see this.

As we know, a page running mocha must have a `<div>` with `id` mocha to show the results. We can add a test using the DOM to check if this `<div>` exists. To do so, add the following test group to your test page:

```
describe('Mocha tests on browser', function() {
    it('should have a div with id mocha', function() {
        assert.isNotNull(document.getElementById('mocha'));
    });
});
```

In this example, we query the DOM for an element with an `id` mocha and use the `asser.isNotNull()` to check if the element exists. As we know the element exists in this page, our tests should pass. If you open this HTML page in your browser you will see this:

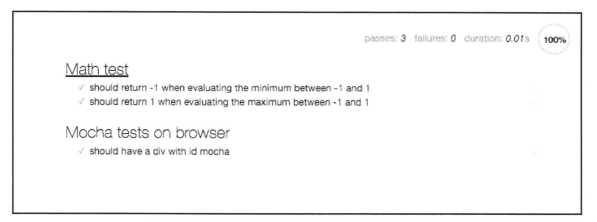

So, all tests are running correctly and we can access the DOM; and now we are ready to create tests for reactive code.

Testing applications using RxJS

When developing using functional reactive programming, you are separating the source of your data from the actions taken when that data is available. This can help test your application, as you can mock your observables to test your observers and keep it independent of your real data source.

To demonstrate this behavior, imagine a program that fetches a web page and extracts all the numbers on that page. We can implement this using regular expressions:

```
var Rx = require('rx');
var request = require('request-promise');
```

```
var parser = {
    getPageObservable: (url)=>Rx.Observable.fromPromise(request(url)),
    parseContentObservable: (observable)=>observable
        .flatMap((str)=>Rx.Observable
        .fromArray(
            str.replace( /\D+/g, ' ').split(' ')
        )
    ).filter((i)=>i!=''),
    getAndParseUrl: function(url){
    var observable = this.getPageObservable(url);
    return this.parseContentObservable(observable);
    }
};

parser
  .getAndParseUrl('http://www.google.com')
  .subscribe((m)=>console.log(m));
module.exports = parser;
```

In this example, we create a `var` called `parser` that contains three methods:

- The first one is called `getPageObservable()`, which fetches a given page.
- The second is `parseContentObservable()`, which replaces all non-number items in the page with a blank space (using a regular expression), and then uses the split method to create an array containing the numbers. We create an `Observable` from that array using the `fromArray()` method, and we `flatMap()` the original `Observable` to create a new `Observable`, which propagates each value individually; finally we use `filter()` to remove all blank strings from the parsed content.
- The third method is called `getAndParseUrl()` and only applies the first two methods. For the last I've added a call to the `getAndParseUrl()` to print it to the console so we can see the result (uncomment this if you want to see it).

If you run this code you will see all numbers in the `http://www.google.com` web page printed in the console.

The first thing to notice is how I've created different methods for each step of the program, and now I can test each one individually. If I want to test the first method, I really have to fetch a page to compare the results, but for the other two methods I can create *fake* observables to compare the results of my tests. A possible test for the `parseContentObservable()` method can be seen in the following code:

```
var assert = require('assert');
var Rx = require('rx');
```

```
var parser = require('./example7_22');

describe('Parser test', function(){
    it('should find the number 123', function(done) {
      var found = false;
      parser.parseContentObservable(
        Rx.Observable.just('some random123 string')
      )
        .subscribe(function(m){
          assert.equal(123,m);
          found = true;
        },
        function(){},
        function(){
          assert.equal(true,found);
          done()
        })
    });
});
```

In this example, we create a test with a random string containing a number. We then subscribe with a `function()`, which enables a flag when called. To the assertion for the number, we use an empty function (`function()`) to listen to errors (you can also fail your test here if you want). For the last, we use a `function()` to be called when the `Observable` finishes. This function asserts the flag was modified and tells mocha that the test is finished (calling the `done()` function). When testing RxJS, you will nearly always be testing asynchronous code, and so you will need to call the `done()` function.

What is really important in our test example is how we can decouple the fetch of a web page and substitute it for a simple observable created with the `just()` method to mock this behavior.

The same pattern can be applied to an observer. As long as you create your observers as independent pieces of code, you will always be able to test it independently of your observables. To demonstrate this, we will implement simple code that creates a `li` element when an observable pushes a new element. To do so we will implement the whole code in the test page as in the following code:

```
<html>
  <head>
    <meta charset="utf-8">
    <title>Tests</title>
    <link href="https://cdn.rawgit.com/mochajs/mocha/2.2.5/mocha.css"
rel="stylesheet" />
  </head>
  <body>
```

```html
    <ul id="container"></ul>
    <div id="mocha"></div>

    <script
src="https://cdn.rawgit.com/mochajs/mocha/2.2.5/mocha.js"></script>
    <script
src="https://cdnjs.cloudflare.com/ajax/libs/chai/3.5.0/chai.min.js"></scrip
t>
    <script
src="https://cdnjs.cloudflare.com/ajax/libs/rxjs/4.1.0/rx.all.min.js"></scr
ipt>
    <script>
var clickObservableFactory = function(element){
        return Rx.Observable.fromEvent(element,'click');
      };

      window.observerFactory = function(){
        return Rx.Observer.create(function(value){
          var node = document.createElement("li");
          var textnode = document.createTextNode("clicked");
          node.appendChild(textnode);
          document.getElementById("container").appendChild(node);
        });
      };
    </script>
    <script>
      mocha.setup('bdd');
      var assert = chai.assert;
      describe('Page test', function() {
        it('should create a li element for each click', function() {
          var observer = window.observerFactory();
          observer.onNext();
          observer.onNext();
    assert.equal(2,document.getElementById('container')
.getElementsByTagName('li').length);
        });
      });
      mocha.run();
    </script>
  </body>
</html>
```

If you open this page on your browser you will see output like the following screenshot:

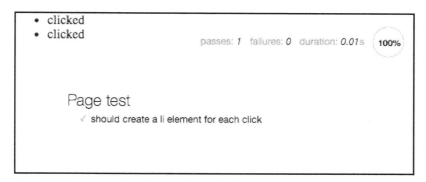

In this code we create the `Observer` using the `create()` method. To test his behavior, we do not need any observable on our program; we just call the `onNext()` method of it and it executes. The same can be done for the `onError()` and `onCompleted()` methods, and this makes it a lot easier to test our application.

> The whole code was placed in the same HTML page so we do not have to use any headless browser to test our code. When we create our example application we will implement tests and use headless browsers to see it running. If you have no experience of this, it will be explained as we go along.

Summary

This chapter was very important as it answered two main questions for any programmer using any program paradigm:

- How can I handle errors in my program?
- How can I better test my program?

From the error perspective, we learned about the default behavior to propagate errors when using reactive extensions for JavaScript, and which operators we can use when we want better control over these errors.

From the test perspective, we learned how we can test our application in the server and in the browser, and the advantage of decoupled applications for testability as it lets us test smaller chunks of code and easily mock others.

In the next chapter, we will look at some operators which don't fit into any of the previous chapters but are still important. We will also review the examples that we have learned so far.

8
More about Operators

In the last chapter, we learned how to handle errors in our reactive applications; we saw that, if we do nothing to handle errors on our observables, that they will be propagated, notifying all the observers of that observable and stopping the observable without ever calling the `onCompleted()` method of the observers. Besides that we learned a set of operators to change this behavior and have more control over errors, as follows:

- `catch()`
- `onErrorResumeNext()`
- `retry()`
- `mergeDelayError()`

These operators give us more control over when to propagate the error and what to do in the event of an error.

Another really important lesson from the last chapter was the implementation of tests for programs using functional reactive programming, as on this paradigm we are always using asynchronous computation and our test needs to be ready to support this behavior.

The nature of functional reactive programming lets us decouple the source of our data from the effects of the occurrence of that data (observables and observers) and we learned how this helps us better architec of our tests, giving us more tools to test smaller chunks of code.

In this chapter, we have the following two main objectives:

- Review some of the lessons of this book using more advanced examples
- Learn more advanced and important operators

We will start reviewing what we have learned so far, since some of the next operators are a little bit harder to understand and some are basically a derivation of other operators; after that we will delve into some new operators.

This chapter will prepare you to be an advanced user of functional reactive programming, after this chapter you will learn how to compose operators and create a client-server chat application using the tools that we have gathered from this book.

So it's really important that you have a good knowledge of what we have learned so far.

The road so far

In previous chapters we learned a lot about functional reactive programming and how we can use it to improve the readability and maintainability of our code; we used two different libraries so:

- `bacon.js`
- `RxJS`

We started with bacon.js because it is simpler to learn and to start creating reactive codes, but after this introduction we explored RxJS as it implements other concepts that we can use to improve our applications.

These two libraries are not the only available libraries for functional reactive programming in JavaScript, but by understanding them, you can probably learn some of the others libraries available with ease.

Another advantage of RxJS over the other libraries for functional reactive programming in JavaScript is its being an implementation of the Rx specification. You can find this implementation for several other languages and platforms such as RxJava and RxSwift for instance, so a good understanding of functional reactive programming and RxJS can improve your code skills in other platforms.

Now, before we go even further into more advanced concepts and examples of RxJS, it's important to make sure that the concepts from the previous chapters created a solid foundation in your mind so we can keep going. Feel free to read some of the chapters or sections again if you do not feel comfortable, and stay alert for the next section as it will contain the most basic information that you must have to create your own programs with functional reactive programming.

The fundamentals of RxJS

In `Chapter 3`, *A World Full of Change - Reactive Extentions to the Rescue,* we learned about observables and observers; these two objects are the most important part of functional reactive programming. Observables are objects with the capacity to listen to events occurring in an environment and they notify other objects of these events; the objects being notified are called observers and they have the capacity to react to the events propagated by an observable. They can listen for up to three events:

- `onNext()`: Triggers when new data is propagated by an observable to this observer
- `onError()`: Triggers when an error is propagated by an observable to this observer
- `onCompleted()`: Triggers when the observable finishes without any error

RxJS gives us the opportunity to create observables from different sources of data using some built-in functions, but it also lets you create custom observables for any source of data you might need.

Subjects are a special class of objects that let you create pushable observables, which means you can add data, errors of finish it at any time.

Another important lesson in this chapter was our first subscription. The observers must subscribe to an observable to listen to the events from this observable creating a subscription; observers can also unsubscribe from an observable at any time if they are no longer interested in events of this observable.

A lot of the power of functional reactive programming comes from the usage of operators. Operators let you interact and modify the data being propagated by an observable before it reaches an observer. Actually, under the hood, every time you call an operator over an observable it does not modify that observable, but creates a new observable instead, which will propagate the modified data. This is really important, as with this behavior, we know that adding an operator to an observable will not change the data propagated by other subscriptions of this observable.

The operators comes with different flavors and they can be used to implement a lot of things. We needed a lot of chapters to explain how some of them work and how they modify the data; for the next sections we will review some of their usage, highlighting the difference between them and also learning new examples of some operators we know. These are the next sections:

- The map() operator versus the flatMap() operator: The difference between these two operators can be subtle, but they are really important; in this section we will see the differences with a lot of examples
- Filtering data: New examples and usage of some operators we already learned to filter data
- Aggregating data: Once again new examples of how we can aggregate the data propagated by an observable
- Going beyond the basics: A closer look at some other really important operators like the ones used to mitigate the problem of back pressure and used to combine observables

 If you already know everything about some of these sections feel free to skip it, but I strongly advise you to take time to read them, to make sure you learned it.

The map() operator versus the flatMap() operator

These two operators are probably the most important and most used operators from functional reactive programming, and for this reason it is really important to know how to differentiate them.

The map() operator lets you pass as a parameter a function that receives as input the data from the observable and returns new data that will be propagated instead. This new data can be of any type. You can see the map() operator in the following example:

```
Rx.Observable
    .of(1,2,3)
    .map((i)=>i+1)
    .subscribe((i)=>console.log(i));
```

This code is really simple and only sums one to each element of the observable and logs them to the console, so running it you will see this output:

2
3
4

You can see a representation of this operation in the following diagram:

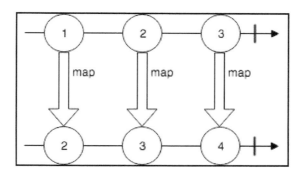

As we discussed, your function can return any type; in our previous example we mapped a number to another number, but let's see what happens if we map a number to a string:

```
Rx.Observable
    .of(1,2,3)
    .map((i)=>'received number => '+i)
    .subscribe((i)=>console.log(i));
```

This code is also really simple and it has no margins for errors, so you probably already know that the output of the execution of this code is as follows:

received number => 1
received number => 2
received number => 3

Yes, really simple, just a string, but what happens if the function I have provided to my `map()` operator returns an `Observable` instead:

```
Rx.Observable
    .of(1,2,3)
    .map((i)=>Rx.Observable.just(i+1))
    .subscribe((i)=>console.log(i));
```

Now the function that we provided to the map() operator returns an Observable with a single value, which is the original value plus 1, and when you run this code you see the following output:

```
JustObservable { _value: 2, _scheduler: ImmediateScheduler {} }
JustObservable { _value: 3, _scheduler: ImmediateScheduler {} }
JustObservable { _value: 4, _scheduler: ImmediateScheduler {} }
```

So it created an observable containing observables; this operation can be described by this diagram:

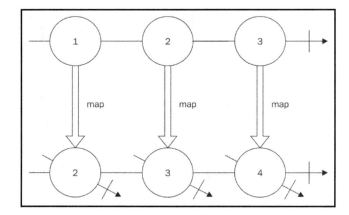

While this is not wrong and can be done, most of the time we are interested in the values of the observables, and at this moment the flatMap() operator comes to the rescue. This operator receives as a parameter a function that maps a given value to an observable, so the return of this function must always be an observable, and this operator will generate a new observable that propagates all values from all observables; it basically maps the values and then flattens your observable of observables.

Here is the same code using flatMap():

```
Rx.Observable
  .of(1,2,3)
  .flatMap((i)=>Rx.Observable.just(i+1))
  .subscribe((i)=>console.log(i));
```

And this code gives you the output you expected:

```
2
3
4
```

And this operation can be described by this diagram:

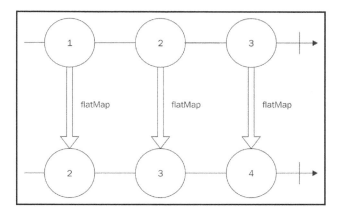

You might be wondering what happens if the function provided to the `flatMap()` operator does not return an observable; let's check it out in the following example:

```
Rx.Observable
    .of(1,2,3)
    .flatMap((i)=>i+1)
    .subscribe((i)=>console.log(i));
```

Well, nothing good can come from this; when running this code an exception will occur and you will end up with a stack trace as shown in following screenshot:

```
X  ~/d/w/1/e/chapter8  node example8_5.js
/Users/ericholiveira/dev/workspace/livro/examplerx/chapter8/node_modules/rx/dist/rx.js:77
    throw e;
    ^

TypeError: innerSource.subscribe is not a function
    at MergeAllObserver.next (/Users/ericholiveira/dev/workspace/livro/examplerx/chapter8/node_modules/rx/dis
t/rx.js:3742:37)
    at MergeAllObserver.Rx.internals.AbstractObserver.AbstractObserver.onNext (/Users/ericholiveira/dev/works
pace/livro/examplerx/chapter8/node_modules/rx/dist/rx.js:1762:31)
    at MergeAllObserver.tryCatcher (/Users/ericholiveira/dev/workspace/livro/examplerx/chapter8/node_modules/
rx/dist/rx.js:63:31)
    at AutoDetachObserverPrototype.next (/Users/ericholiveira/dev/workspace/livro/examplerx/chapter8/node_mod
ules/rx/dist/rx.js:5883:51)
    at AutoDetachObserver.Rx.internals.AbstractObserver.AbstractObserver.onNext (/Users/ericholiveira/dev/wor
kspace/livro/examplerx/chapter8/node_modules/rx/dist/rx.js:1762:31)
    at InnerObserver.Rx.FlatMapObservable.InnerObserver.next (/Users/ericholiveira/dev/workspace/livro/exampl
erx/chapter8/node_modules/rx/dist/rx.js:2145:14)
    at InnerObserver.Rx.internals.AbstractObserver.AbstractObserver.onNext (/Users/ericholiveira/dev/workspac
e/livro/examplerx/chapter8/node_modules/rx/dist/rx.js:1762:31)
    at InnerObserver.tryCatcher (/Users/ericholiveira/dev/workspace/livro/examplerx/chapter8/node_modules/rx/
dist/rx.js:63:31)
    at AutoDetachObserverPrototype.next (/Users/ericholiveira/dev/workspace/livro/examplerx/chapter8/node_mod
ules/rx/dist/rx.js:5883:51)
    at AutoDetachObserver.Rx.internals.AbstractObserver.AbstractObserver.onNext (/Users/ericholiveira/dev/wor
kspace/livro/examplerx/chapter8/node_modules/rx/dist/rx.js:1762:31)
```

And this is wrong for sure.

So keep in mind that the function provided to the `map()` operator can return any type, and if you return an observable, it will create an observable of observables, while the function provided to the `flatMap()` operator must always return an observable.

We can use operators to emulate other operators, and `flatMap()` is really powerful as you can use it to emulate a lot of different operators; as an example, let's emulate the `filter()` operator using only the `flatMap()` operator.

Challenge - Creating a function to filter elements using only the flatMap() operator

To show how powerful the `flatMap()` operator can be we can create a function to emulate the `filter()` operator using only the `flatMap()` operator; this function must have the following signature:

```
filterUsingFlatMap(observable, filter);
```

It will receive two parameters and both are mandatory:

- `observable`: It is the observable to filter data
- `filter`: It is a function that chooses if an element should be filtered or not

And it must return an observable for the filter.

Before coding our function, let's create a test suite to test it.

Let's use mocha as we learned in the previous chapter. We can define our test group using the `describe()` function:

```
var assert = require('assert');
var Rx = require('rx');
var filterUsingFlatMap = require('./example8_6');
describe('Test for filter function', function() {
 //Test goes here
});
```

In this code we imported the `assert` module and `Rx` module, the first to do the assertion for our tests and the other to create observables to test. The third module contains the function we want to test; this function is contained in a file called `example8_6` (which can be downloaded from the website). I will also put the implementation of it here.

The `describe()` function creates a group of tests for our implementation, I designed four tests; they are not exhaustive and you can surely come up with more tests to make sure the implementation is correct.

The first test ensures that when an empty `observable` is passed as an argument to the `filter()` function, the observable returned from this function won't emit any data; it can be seen in the following code:

```
it('should not propagate any data if the observable is empty',
function(done) {
    var eventCalled = false;
    var observable = Rx.Observable.empty();
    filterUsingFlatMap(observable,function noop(){})
      .subscribe(
        function(){eventCalled=true},
        function(){eventCalled=true},
        function(){
          assert.equal(eventCalled,false);
          done();
        }
      )
});
```

For this test we have to make sure that the `onNext()` and the `onError()` events are never called. To test it I decided to create a flag (`eventCalled`), and change the value of this flag whenever the result observable emits any of these events. We then create an empty observable and pass it as an argument to the `filterUsingFlatMap()` function; we also add an `empty()` function as we are not interested in it in our test, and an `onCompleted()` function to assert that the flag has not changed and to finish our test calling the `done()` function.

The next test ensures that the data is propagated when our `filter()` function returns `true`, and it can be seen in this code:

```
it('must propagates all the data if the filter function always returns
true', function(done) {
    var counter=0,elements = [1,2];
    var observable = Rx.Observable.fromArray(elements);
    filterUsingFlatMap(observable,function(){return true;})
      .subscribe(
        function(){counter++;},
        function noop(){},
        function(){
          assert.equal(counter,elements.length);
          done();
        }
```

```
        )
});
```

For this test we add a counter to count the number of elements propagated and sum 1 to this counter whenever the onNext() method is called; we also create an array (elements) and an observable from it, and in our onCompleted() method we make sure that the counter is equal to the number of elements in our array (this ensures that all data was propagated) and finishes the test.

The third test does the exact opposite, making sure that all data is filtered when our filter() function returns false, and it can be seen in this code:

```
it('should not propagate any data if the filter function always return
false',function(done){
    var counter=0,elements = [1,2];
    var observable = Rx.Observable.fromArray(elements);
    filterUsingFlatMap(observable,function(){return false;})
      .subscribe(
        function(){counter++;},
        function noop(){},
        function(){
          assert.equal(counter,0);
          done();
        }
      );
});
```

This test is really similar to the last; the only change is it expects the counter to be zero (which means no data was propagated).

For the last test we take an array and filter the even numbers, its implementation can be seen in the following code:

```
it('must respect the filter',function(done){
    var counter=0,elements = [1,2];
    var elementFound;
    var observable = Rx.Observable.fromArray(elements);
    filterUsingFlatMap(observable,function(i){return i % 2===0;})
      .subscribe(
        function(i){
          counter++;
          elementFound=i;
        },
        function noop(){},
        function(){
          assert.equal(counter,1);
          assert.equal(elementFound,2);
```

```
            done();
        }
    )
});
```

Here we changed our `filter()` function, to return `true` for even numbers and `false` for odd numbers; we also store the element that we found in a variable and, as the only even number in this array is the number 2, we expect the counter to be equal to 1 and the element found to be equal to 2.

Now that we have our tests we are ready to implement our `filter()` function using only `flatMap()`; a good practice is to always fail your tests before trying the real implementation, so let's try the following implementation for our `filter()` function:

```
var Rx = require('rx');
module.exports = function(observable, filter){
return observable;
};
```

On our first attempt to implement the `filter()` function we are just returning the own `observable`, so some of our tests must fail. If we run our tests this is what happens:

```
[bash-3.2$ mocha example8_6_test.js

Test for filter function
  ✓ should not propagate any data if the observable is empty
  ✓ must propagates all the data if the filter function always returns true
  1) should not propagate any data if the filter function always return false
  2) must respect the filter


  2 passing (16ms)
  2 failing

  1) Test for filter function should not propagate any data if the filter function always return false:

      AssertionError: 2 == 0
      + expected - actual

      -2
      +0

      at AnonymousObserver._onCompleted (example8_6_test.js:39:18)
      at AnonymousObserver.Rx.AnonymousObserver.AnonymousObserver.completed (node_modules/rx/dist/rx.js:1843:12)
      at AnonymousObserver.Rx.internals.AbstractObserver.AbstractObserver.onCompleted (node_modules/rx/dist/rx.js:1782:14)
      at AnonymousObserver.tryCatcher (node_modules/rx/dist/rx.js:63:31)
      at AutoDetachObserverPrototype.completed (node_modules/rx/dist/rx.js:5897:56)
      at AutoDetachObserver.Rx.internals.AbstractObserver.AbstractObserver.onCompleted (node_modules/rx/dist/rx.js:1782:14)
      at loopRecursive (node_modules/rx/dist/rx.js:2763:13)
      at scheduleWork [as action] (node_modules/rx/dist/rx.js:985:11)
      at ScheduledItem.invokeCore (node_modules/rx/dist/rx.js:896:33)
      at ScheduledItem.invoke (node_modules/rx/dist/rx.js:884:40)
      at runTrampoline (node_modules/rx/dist/rx.js:1125:37)
      at tryCatcher (node_modules/rx/dist/rx.js:63:31)
      at CurrentThreadScheduler.schedule (node_modules/rx/dist/rx.js:1141:45)
      at FromArrayObservable.Rx.ObservableBase.ObservableBase._subscribe (node_modules/rx/dist/rx.js:2095:32)
      at FromArrayObservable.Rx.Observable.observableProto.subscribe.observableProto.forEach (node_modules/rx/dist/rx.js:2034:19)
      at Context.<anonymous> (example8_6_test.js:35:8)

  2) Test for filter function must respect the filter:

      AssertionError: 2 == 1
      + expected - actual

      -2
      +1

      at AnonymousObserver._onCompleted (example8_6_test.js:56:18)
      at AnonymousObserver.Rx.AnonymousObserver.AnonymousObserver.completed (node_modules/rx/dist/rx.js:1843:12)
      at AnonymousObserver.Rx.internals.AbstractObserver.AbstractObserver.onCompleted (node_modules/rx/dist/rx.js:1782:14)
      at AnonymousObserver.tryCatcher (node_modules/rx/dist/rx.js:63:31)
```

Two tests passed: the test that checks if no data is propagated when the observable is empty and the one that checks if all data is propagated when the filter() function returns true; as we are returning the own observable it makes sense that both of these tests were accepted, but two of our tests failed, as can be seen in the previous screenshot.

Now let's try to implement our function using only the flatMap() operator. The filter() function must propagate the data when the filter() returns true, and it must omit when it returns false; we can easily propagate the data using flatMap() if we return an observable using the just() method:

```
var Rx = require('rx');
module.exports = function(observable,filter){
    return observable.flatMap(
        (data)=>Rx.Observable.just(data)
    );
};
```

We do not even need to test it, as we know it will fail; we need to find a way to omit the data based on the given filter.

How can we omit data using flatMap()?

The answer is simple. We can return an observable created with the method empty. Observables created with this method are empty so they are going to omit the data in the results. The final part is to execute the filter() function to decide if we must propagate the data.

The final code for the function using only the flatMap() operator is as follows:

```
var Rx = require('rx');
module.exports = function(observable,filter){
    return observable.flatMap(
        (data)=>{
          if(filter(data)){
            return Rx.Observable.just(data);
          }else{
            return Rx.Observable.empty();
          }
        }
    );
};
```

So we call the `filter()` function passing the data, and if the result is a truthy value we return an observable containing only this data; otherwise we return an empty observable omitting the data from the result.

If we execute our tests on this new function we will see this output:

```
[bash-3.2$ mocha example8_6_test.js


Test for filter function
  ✓ should not propagate any data if the observable is empty
  ✓ must propagates all the data if the filter function always returns true
  ✓ should not propagate any data if the filter function always return false
  ✓ must respect the filter


4 passing (15ms)
```

Now our tests works, as we expected, and we just implemented a `filter()` function using only the `flatMap()` operator.

> Feel free to implement more tests to it as an exercise.

Filtering data

We learned about some different operators to filter data from an observable; the `filter()` operator is probably the most common and useful. When using this operator you must provide a function to be used as a filter for each element propagated by the observable; the return of this function will be used to decide if the data should be propagated or not, and this is what happens when the result of the function is evaluated, if the result is:

- A truthy value: the object is propagated
- A falsy value: the object is omitted
- The falsy values are:
    - False
    - Null
    - Undefined

- 0
  - NaN (not a number)
  - "" (empty string)
- The truthy values are:
  - Any non-falsy value

So when you see the following code:

```
Rx.Observable
  .interval(100)
  .filter(
    (i)=> i%3
  )
  .take(4)
  .subscribe((i)=>console.log(i));
```

What values will be printed in the console?

1. 3,6,9,12

2. 1,2,4,5

3. 1,2,4

4. 3

The correct answer is option 2, that is:

```
1
2
4
5
```

This happens because we first created an observable that generates consecutive numbers with the `interval()` function; we then created a new observable containing filtered data from this observable. The `filter()` function uses the `%` operator over the value, this operator returns the rest of the division by the given number, so in our example the `filter()` function returns the rest of the division between the number and three, this function will return 0 for multiples of 3 and 1 or 2 otherwise, 0 is a falsy value and 1 and 2 are truthy values, so the multiples of 3 are omitted; we then create an observable from this containing only four elements with the `take()` operator.

All these operators create an observable containing the first four natural numbers that are not multiples of 3, for this reason, option 2 (1,2,4, and 5), is the correct answer.

Aggregating data

The most important operator to aggregate data is the reduce() operator, as the other operators the reduce() operator returns a new observable; in this case the observable returned contains a single value that is the result of the execution of a function over all the elements of the original observable.

We can use the reduce() operator to find the lower numeric value in an observable:

```
Rx.Observable
  .of(1,5,0,9,56,-2,13)
  .reduce(function(a,b){
    if(a<b){
      return a;
    }else{
      return b;
    }
  })
  .subscribe((i)=>console.log(i));
```

In this example, the values from the observable are going to be scanned from left to right, and the reduce() function is used to check which one is lower (the if/else block), and then we log the result. Thus, as expected the result is:

-2

 The reduce() operator can be used for mathematical operations; actually, RxJS contains some mathematical operators such as min, max, and sum and each one can be easily implemented using the reduce() operator. You can also use the reduce() operator for other operations such as creating an array, a new object, concatenating strings, and so on; every time you need to aggregate data the reduce() operator can be your ally.

Going beyond the basics

RxJS supplies a lot more than just operators to do simple transformation in your data, we learned some more complex usages for it and we will review the most important of it.

Dealing with backpressure

Backpressure happens every time you receive data faster than you are able to process for a given time.

Before even starting to code your solution for back pressure you must decide if you are willing to spend memory or lose data.

When you can lose data you can use a lossy strategy; the advantage of this strategy is it has a low consumption of memory, and lets you mitigate the problem using constant memory. The lossy operators that we learned are as follows:

- `throttle()`
- `sample()`
- `debounce()`
- `pausable()`

If you cannot lose data, you can use memory to store data while processing it; the strategy you will use to deal with backpressure is the loss-less strategy. We learned the following operators to loss-less operators to deal with backpressure:

- `bufferWithCount()`
- `bufferWithTime()`
- `bufferWithTimeOrCount()`
- `pausableBuffered()`
- `controlled()`

Knowing the limits of your program (memory or data) will help you to decide what operators to use.

Combining observables

The most important thing is to remember that you can even combine observables to create a new one using data from both.

There are three really important operators for this:

- merge()
- concat()
- zip()

The concat() operator generates a new observable containing the data from all provided observables; the data is propagated on the new observable following the order of the observables, so it first propagates all the data from the first observable, and only after it finishes does it go to the next and so on. One important thing is that, if one observable is infinite (and for this reason never finishes), it never goes to the next.

The merge() operator is similar to the concat() operator, but it follows the order of the values, so it listens for data in all observables and propagates it to the created observable as soon as it occurs. When using this operator even if one of the observables is infinite it propagates the data from all.

The zip() operator is a little bit different from the other two, as it creates a new observable from a combination of the other observables; by default it propagates an array containing the values from each of them, but you can also provide a function to combine them as you want.

 So that is our quick review summarizing some of the most important lessons from this book up to this point; feel free to review your weaknesses. In this chapter, we will learn some other advanced operators.

Other important operators

Some important operators from RxJS don't have a perfect match with the groups of operators we learned so far, but they can easily solve some complex and specific problems with a few lines of code, making you feel like a magician when using them. Now we are going to learn them.

The flatMapLatest() operator

This operator is similar to the flatMap() operator, but it only propagates items from the most recently transformed observable.

Imagine a *search as you type* feature. In this feature, for every key stroke you will do a search and present the current result in the screen; if you are accessing external resources such as a database or an API, some searches can take more time than others, and the naive implementation of this search (using `flatMap()` for instance) might show wrong results. Look at this example:

1. A search box to search names in a database.
2. The user types the letter J and starts a search for all available names starting with the letter J.
3. The user types the letter O and starts a search for all available names starting with JO.
4. The search for names starting with JO finishes and presents the results (John and Joe, for instance).
5. The first search (names starting with J) finally finishes (it took more time than the search for JO), and changes the presented results using names starting with J (Jean, June, John, for instance).
6. The presented results are wrong, because the user search box shows JO , and some of the presented results do not start with JO (Jean and June).

The `flatMapLatest()` operator is perfect for this case, as in the presented example the results for J would be discarded in case it took more time to finish.

The `flatMapLatest()` operator has the following signature:

```
observable.flatMapLatest(selectorFunction, [selectorContext]);
```

It receives up to two parameters; the first is mandatory and the second is optional:

- `selectorFunction`: It is a function that maps a value to an observable sequence
- `selectorContext`: In the `this` parameter (context) used in the `selectorFunction`

An example usage of this operator can be seen in the following code:

```
Rx.Observable
  .of(1,2,3)
  .flatMapLatest(
    (i)=>Rx.Observable.just(i+1)
  ).subscribe((k)=>console.log(k));
```

This example is simple and it works the same way the flatMap() operator works; it will give you the following output:

2
3
4

We can implement the search as you type feature to see the difference; for this let's create an HTML page with the implementation and compare the result:

```html
<html>
  <head></head>
  <body>

    <input type="text" id="my_input"/>
    <button id="my_button">Search</button>
    <span id="my_span"></span>

    <script
src="https://cdnjs.cloudflare.com/ajax/libs/rxjs/4.1.0/rx.all.js"></script>

    <script>
      var enterKeyUpObservable = Rx.Observable
        .fromEvent(document.getElementById("my_input"),"keyup")
        .flatMap(function(e){
          var value = document.getElementById("my_input").value;
          return Rx.Observable
            .just("results for: "+value)
            .delay(Math.max((10 - value.length)*1000,100));
        });

      enterKeyUpObservable.subscribe(function(text){
        document.getElementById('my_span').innerHTML = text;
      });
    </script>
  </body>
</html>
```

This HTML page will expose a search box, and as you type in it it will do a fake search, showing the value used in the search as text; we are using the flatMap() operator to emulate the search feature, and we use a delay to emulate the time taken to execute the search, if you run this HTML page and type something in the search box you will see the following screenshot:

It is showing the results for the letter **s** alone, but we wanted the result for all the given input; to fix this, all we have to do is use the `flatMapLatest()` operator instead. Use the following code:

```
var enterKeyUpObservable = Rx.Observable
    .fromEvent(document.getElementById("my_input"),"keyup")
    .flatMapLatest(function(e){
      var value = document.getElementById("my_input").value;
      return Rx.Observable
        .just("results for: "+value)
        .delay(Math.max((10 - value.length)*1000,100));
    });
```

You will see an HTML page like this instead:

The flatMapFirst() operator

This operator propagates data from the first mapped observable, and it only goes to the next when it finishes discarding all the other observables before finishing.

The `flatMapFirst()` operator has the following signature:

```
observable.flatMapFirst(selectorFunction,[selectorContext]);
```

It receives up to two parameters; the first is mandatory and the second is optional:

- `selectorFunction`: It is a function that maps a value to an observable sequence
- `selectorContext`: In this parameter (context) used in the `selectorFunction`

An example usage of this operator can be seen in the following code:

```
Rx.Observable
  .interval(50)
  .flatMapFirst(
    (i)=>Rx.Observable.interval(30)
      .map((k)=>'running for: '+i+' flatMapFirst: '+k)
      .take(3)
  ).subscribe((i)=>console.log(i));
```

In this example we create an `Observable` from an `interval()`; this observable will emit consecutive integers starting from zero every `50` milliseconds. We use `flatMapFirst()` to map it to an observable also created from an `interval()` to generate a string (this string is only for a debug purposes, to show which value from the original observable is running), we then take three items (to make sure it finishes and can go to the next) and subscribe to them.

If you run this code you will see the following output:

```
running for: 0 flatMapFirst: 0
running for: 0 flatMapFirst: 1
running for: 0 flatMapFirst: 2
running for: 3 flatMapFirst: 0
running for: 3 flatMapFirst: 1
running for: 3 flatMapFirst: 2
running for: 5 flatMapFirst: 0
running for: 5 flatMapFirst: 1
//keeps printing until we stop the program
```

By looking at the output it is easier to understand how this operator works; it started to run for the value 0 (the first value propagated from the original observable), and propagates all elements from the flatMapped observable (the first three strings in the format `running for: 0 flatMapFirst: X`). It drops all values propagated while the observable from the `flatMapFirst()` is running; for this reason the values 1 and 2 are discarded and it goes to the next value, the value 3, and the execution repeats.

 There is an alias for this operator called `selectSwitchFirst`.

The finally() operator

This operator is simple and useful, and works similarly to the `finally` from the `try/catch/finally` block. It executes a specified function after the original observable finishes (even in the case of failure).

It has the following signature:

```
observable.finally(action);
```

It receives only one parameter and it is mandatory:

- `action`: It is the function to be executed when the original observable finishes, even in the case of failure

This operator is simple and two examples are enough to understand it.

The first example shows its usage in an observable finishing gracefully:

```
Rx.Observable
  .just(1)
  .finally(()=>console.log('FINALLY'))
  .subscribe((i)=>console.log(i));
```

If you run this code you will see the following output, showing the provided `finally` function being executed after the observable finishes:

```
1
FINALLY
```

The other example shows the behavior of this operator in the case of failure:

```
Rx.Observable
  .throw(new Error('ERROR'))
  .finally(()=>console.log('FINALLY'))
  .subscribe((i)=>console.log(i));
```

In this case, an error occurred in our observable, and if you run this code you will see the following output, showing the provided `finally()` function being executed after the observable finishes:

```
~/d/w/l/e/chapter8 [?]node example8_14.js
FINALLY
/Users/ericholiveira/dev/workspace/livro/examplerx/chapter8/node_modules/rx/dist/rx.js:77
    throw e;
    ^

Error: ERROR
    at Object.<anonymous> (/Users/ericholiveira/dev/workspace/livro/examplerx/chapter8/example8_14.js:4:10)
    at Module._compile (module.js:541:32)
    at Object.Module._extensions..js (module.js:550:10)
    at Module.load (module.js:458:32)
    at tryModuleLoad (module.js:417:12)
    at Function.Module._load (module.js:409:3)
    at Module.runMain (module.js:575:10)
    at run (node.js:348:7)
    at startup (node.js:140:9)
    at node.js:463:3
```

The groupBy() operator

This operator lets you group the values of an observable sequence. It will generate an observable containing an observable for each group.

It has the following signature:

```
observable.groupBy(groupFunction, [valueSelector]);
```

It receives two parameters, the first mandatory and the second optional:

- `groupFunction`: It is the function to decide which group a value belongs to
- `valueSelector`: It is a function to select the value to be propagated; if none is specified, it propagates its own value

A simple example usage of this operator would be two odd and even numbers apart in an observable sequence:

```
Rx.Observable
  .of(0,1,2,3,4,5)
  .groupBy((i)=>i%2)
  .subscribe((obs)=>{
    obs.toArray().subscribe((arr)=>console.log(arr))
});
```

In this example, we use the `groupBy()` operator to take even and odd numbers apart, as it generates an observable for each group, the parameter received by the `subscription` function is an observable, we then turn it into an observable containing only an array and log it; so if we run this code, we will see printed in the console an array of even numbers and an array of odd numbers:

```
[ 0, 2, 4 ]
[ 1, 3, 5 ]
```

Another example usage of this operator using that second parameter would be to group names by the first letter:

```
Rx.Observable
  .of(
    {name:'Mary',lastName:'Jane'},
    {name:'John',lastName:'Doe'},
    {name:'Jean',lastName:'Carter'},
    {name:'Erich',lastName:'Oliveira'})
  .groupBy(
    (person)=>person.name[0],
    (person)=>person.name+' '+person.lastName
```

```
).flatMap(
    (personObservable)=>personObservable.toArray()
).map(
    (arr)=>'Names starting with '+arr[0][0]+': '+arr.join()
).subscribe((str)=>console.log(str));
```

This example is a little bit more complex. We create an `Observable` from objects containing the first name and last name of four people, we then use `groupBy()` to group them by the first letter of their name and map the object to a string containing the name and last name (the second parameter of `groupBy()`); the result is an observable of observables. We then `flatMap()` it to transform it into an observable of arrays; we finally map those arrays to a string containing their first letter and all the names in the array and log it.

If you run this code, you will see the following output:

```
Names starting with M: Mary Jane
Names starting with J: John Doe,Jean Carter
Names starting with E: Erich Oliveira
```

The do() operator

This operator lets you execute arbitrary functions; it is really useful for debugging purposes, as you can log the data and have a better understanding of the workflow of your observable.

It has the following signature:

```
observable.do(execute);
```

It receives only one parameter and it is mandatory:

- `execute`: It is the function to be executed by this observable, it receives the value propagated by the observable as a parameter

An example usage of this operator can be seen in the following code:

```
Rx.Observable
    .of('Joe DiMaggio','Friedrich Nietzsche','Nayara Neves','Marco Antonio')

    .map((name)=>name.split(' ')[1])
    .do((data)=>console.log('[DEBUG] Data after map operator: '+data))
```

```
.filter((name)=>name.indexOf('N')===0)
.do((data)=>console.log('[DEBUG] Data after filter operator:'+data))

.subscribe((result)=>console.log(result));
```

In this example, we create an Observable with some names; we then use the
map() operator to propagate the last name of each person. As we want to trace the execution
we use the do() operator to log the values after the usage of the operator; the do() operator
does not change the data propagated by the observables. We then filter to keep only the last
names starting with the character N; we add do() again to keep tracing the data, and finally
subscribe to it.

If we run this code you will see the following output in your console:

```
[DEBUG] Data after map operator: DiMaggio
[DEBUG] Data after map operator: Nietzsche
[DEBUG] Data after filter operator: Nietzsche
Nietzsche
[DEBUG] Data after map operator: Neves
[DEBUG] Data after filter operator:Neves
Neves
[DEBUG] Data after map operator: Antonio
```

Looking at this result you can understand how the execution happens step by step. It first
propagated the name Joe DiMaggio, mapped it to DiMaggio, and filtered it. As it does not
start with the character N, it does not keep being propagated. Then it goes to the name
Friedrich Nietzsche, which is propagated until the end; the same applies to the names
Nayara Neves and Marco Antonio.

Notice that if we remove the do() operator:

```
Rx.Observable
  .of('Joe DiMaggio','Friedrich Nietzsche','Nayara Neves','Marco Antonio')
  .map((name)=>name.split(' ')[1])
  .filter((name)=>name.indexOf('N')===0)
  .subscribe((result)=>console.log(result));
```

We get the following output:

```
Nietzsche
Neves
```

Which is exactly the same output (removing the debug info), showing that the do() operator never changes the values from the observable.

 There are two aliases for this operator called tap and doAction.

Summary

In this chapter, we started a review of the most important concepts we have learned so far and also revisited some common misconceptions about functional reactive programming and reactive extensions.

In our review, we learned the difference between map() and flatMap(), the power of the flatMap() operator, filtering data and falsy/truthy values, aggregating data, strategies to deal with backpressure, and combining observables.

Elsewhere in this chapter, we learned some new operators such as flatMapLatest(), flatMapFirst(), finally(), groupBy(), and do().

We have already learned how to combine observables; in the next chapter we will learn a new concept called a transducer. Transducers let us combine operators, which improves readability and reuse, helping us to write clearer and more concise applications using functional reactive programming.

9
Composition

In the last chapter, we reviewed some of the key concepts from functional reactive programming using RxJS, including:

- Which events an observable propagates
- What are observables?
- Review of some important operators:
    - Differences between the `map()` and `flatMap()` operators
    - A challenge to emulate an operator from another
    - Filter data
    - Aggregate data

- Tests for an RxJS program
- Mitigating the problem of backpressure
- Combining observables

Paying attention to this review is crucial to have a better and clearer understanding of functional reactive programming, and with this knowledge we are more prepared for more advanced topics, such as some operators from the last chapter:

- `flatMapLatest()`
- `flatMapFirst()`
- `finally()`
- `groupBy()`
- `do()`

In this chapter, we will learn a final topic before we move on to our final project. Using all the knowledge from this book, we already learned how we can combine observables, and now we will learn how we can compose transformations independently using a new concept called a transducer.

What is a transducer?

Transducers are composable algorithmic transformations; they provide a way to compose your operators to create a new one. They are independent of the input source and the output, and for this reason they can be applied not only to observables, but also to arrays, streams, and collections.

The transducers let you describe the operations you want to apply to an input source, this way you can create a pipeline of operations to be applied to them, without ever creating any intermediate aggregation.

You probably remember from previous chapters that, every time we apply an operator to an observable we create a new observable, so if we apply two operators to an observable we will create two extra observables, if we apply three operators to an observable we will create three extra observables, and so on. This does not happen with transducers, because you first describe all the transformations you want to apply to a source of data, so there is no need to create any intermediate observable and this leads to a performance improvement in your code.

Another advantage of using a transducer is the additional layer of abstraction it adds to your code, letting you describe how you can transform your data before even knowing which type of data you are going to use. This extra layer of abstraction lets you reuse more code and also test your transformations independently.

So the main advantages of using transducers are as follows:

- Performance improvements as it avoids the creation of intermediary forms of observable (or any other object being iterated)
- Improves your code maintainability with:
    - Improved testability as it lets you test your transformation independently
    - Improved reuse as it lets you describe the transformation you want to apply to the source of your data and lets you reuse it in other sources

- Improved readability as it lets you describe your transformation, adding more semantic to your code

To use transducers in your code you will need to add another dependency, a library that implements the transducer; currently there are two important libraries supported by RxJS, and they are as follows:

- `transducers-js`: https: //github.com/cognitect-labs/transducers-js
- `transducers.js`: https://github.com/jlongster/transducers.js

Another important thing to notice is, as transducers are input source–agnostic they do not have available all the operators we learned in RxJS. Actually, whichever implementation you choose, contains only a few of them.

The word transducer comes from the combination of the words transform and reduce.

Available transducer implementations for JavaScript

As we seen in the last section, there are two important implementations available, and as transducers libraries implement a protocol, it should be easy to switch implementations. To show example usages of transducers we need to choose one of them, and I will choose to use `transducers-js`; as both are more or less equally popular, but transducers-js has more transformations available, so it should be more easy for you to try, test, and play with a little bit.

Both implementations can be used in both node and browser. In this chapter, we will use it only in node, and to use it all we have to do is to install it using npm:

```
npm install transducers-js
```

In this book, we will be using version 0.4.174 of the `transducers-js` library; to install this specific version run the following command instead:

```
npm install transducers-js@0.4.174
```

The transducers-js API

Before we learn how we can use transducers-js with RxJS, it is important to know which transformations we have available in this library. As we have already learned most of these transformations in RxJS, here is a quick overview of some of the transformations available in the `transducers-js` library API and what each one does:

- transducers.complement (function): It takes a function and returns its complements (negates the result of the function call).
- transducers.filter (function): It takes a function and filters the data based on the result of calling this function over it.
- transducers.first(): It returns the first input.
- transducers.map (function): It uses the given function to map each value into another.
- transducers.partitionAll (integer): It maps the inputs into arrays of a given size.
- transducers.reduce (function, initialObject, iterable): It receives as a parameter a function, an initial value, and the iterable object to be reduced. It returns the reduction of the given iterable object starting with the initial value and applying the given function.
- transducers.remove (function): It is similar to the `filter()` operation, but it removes the value when the given function returns a truthy value.
- transducers.take (integer): It returns an iterable object containing the first *n* items where n is the integer passed as a parameter to the `take()` function.
- transducers.takeWhile (function) : It returns all elements while the given function returns true.

> This is not an exhaustive list of the available methods, but it contains a good portion of them, just enough to get us started with transducers. All available methods can be found in the link `http://cognitect-labs.github.io/transducers-js/classes/trans ducers.html`.

Using transducers

As we discussed in previous sections, transducers are a way to compose algorithmic transformations over iterable objects; to see this in action, let's first use a transducer in the most simple iterable object, an array.

To run a transducer over an array we first need a method to run a given transformation in a given iterable object.

For this we use the `into()` method, which has the following signature:

```
transducers.into(emptyIterable,transformation,iterable)
```

It receives three parameters and they are all mandatory:

- `emptyIterable`: It is an empty iterable used to store the result of the application of the transformation over the iterable object
- `transformation`: It is the function or transducers to be applied over the `iterable` object
- `iterable`: It is the `iterable` object to be transformed

With the usage of this function we can implement transformations over an array, let's see how we can implement a simple map with it:

```
var t = require('transducers-js');

var iterableObject = [1,2,3,4];
var mapTransducer = t.map((i)=>i+1);

var result = t.into(
  [],
  mapTransducer,
  iterableObject
);

console.log(result);
```

This example does the following:

1. Imports the `transducers-js` library and stores it in the `t` variable.
2. Creates an array called `iterableObject`, where the transformation will be applied; the array contains the value `[1,2,3,4]`.
3. Creates a transducer to map the values of an `iterable` object in it plus one, called `mapTransducer`.
4. Calls the into method to iterate the `iterableObject` using the `mapTransducer` into an empty array passed as the first argument of the method; the result of this is stored in the `result` variable.

5. Logs to the console the `result` variable; this step prints the value `[ 2, 3, 4, 5 ]` in the console, as we expect.

This is a simple example, showing a simple transformation over an array, but with transducers we can compose several transformations to be applied over an `iterable` object. The composition itself is done using the `comp ()` method; this method has the following signature:

```
transducers.comp(...transfomations)
```

It receives an arbitrary number of arguments, each one being a transformation to be applied on the `iterable` object.

To see this method in action, let's implement a transducer using the `map` and `filter` transformations to calculate sum one to each number in an `iterable` object and filter to keep only the even numbers:

```
var t = require('transducers-js');
var iterableObject = [1,2,3,4];

var mapTransducer = t.map((i)=>i+1);
var filterTransducer = t.filter((i)=>i%2===0);

var composedTransducer = t.comp(mapTransducer,filterTransducer);

var result = t.into(
    [],
    composedTransducer,
    iterableObject
);

console.log(result);
```

This new code creates our first composition of transformations, with the following steps:

1. Imports the `transducers-js` library and stores it in the `t` variable.
2. Creates an array called `iterableObject`, where the transformation will be applied, the array contains the value `[1,2,3,4]`.
3. Creates a transducer to map the values of an `iterable` object in it plus one, called `mapTransducer`.
4. Creates a transducer to filter the values of an `iterable` object keeping only the even numbers, called `filterTransducer`.

5. Creates a composition of transformations, respecting order of the parameters from left to right, so the first applies the `map()` transformation and then the `filter()` transformation, called `composedTransducer`.

6. Calls the `into()` method to iterate the `iterableObject` using the `composedTransducer` into an empty array passed as the first argument of the method; the result of this is stored in the `result` variable.

7. Logs to the console the `result` variable; this step prints the value [2, 4] in the console, as we expect.

 Remember that the order is important, so when we run the map transformation over the `iterable` object [1,2,3,4] the result is the sum of each number with one [2,3,4,5] and then we filter to keep only the even numbers [2,4], as seen in the output.

If we switch the orders of the parameters passed to `t.comp` we first apply `filter` and the `map`, so we would first filter only the even numbers; then, applying the `map` transformation that sums 1 to each value, on the previous code we changed the order of this line:

```
var composedTransducer = t.comp(filterTransducer,mapTransducer);
```

Running the code with this change gives us a different output:

```
[ 3, 5 ]
```

When we run with this small change we must first filter the array ([1, 2, 3, 4) to keep only the even numbers ([2, 4]), and then map it to its value plus 1, which gives use the output [3, 5].

Using transducers with RxJS

In the last section, we learned how we can apply a transducer to the most simple `iterable` object in JavaScript, an array. But we are more interested in how we can use this tool in functional reactive programming using RxJS.

Using transducers with RxJS we can see performance improvements, as we will avoid the creation of intermediate observable sequences and can improve the overall quality of our code with the composition of transformations.

To use a transducer in RxJS we need to use the transduce operator of the RxJS library; this operator has the following signature:

```
observable.transduce(transducer)
```

It receives only one mandatory argument:

- `transducer`: It is the transducer transformation to be applied on the observable sequence

The transduce operator, like any other observable operator, returns a new operator, but as we can compose several transformations inside a single transducer we will create only one new observable.

 Imagine an observable where we apply two operators, the `filter()` operator and the `map()` operator, for each operator applied. RxJS creates a new intermediate observable, creating two new observables. If we decide to create a transducer composing both transformations instead, RxJS would create only one extra observable, and this leads to a performance improvement; we will see in the benchmark section of this chapter the performance improvement of the transducers approach.

Now let's see an example usage of transducers with observable sequences. First let's implement a simple map using transducers:

```
var t = require('transducers-js');
var Rx = require('rx');

var mapTransducer = t.map((i)=>i+1);
Rx.Observable
  .of(1,2,3,4)
  .transduce(mapTransducer)
  .subscribe((i)=>console.log(i));
```

Here we simply create a `mapTransducer` to sum one to each value of an `iterable` object, we then create an `Observable` containing four values, apply the transduce operator using the `mapTransducer` over it, and finally subscribe to `log` the content of this observable sequence.

The execution of this code gives us the following output:

```
2
3
4
5
```

The code can be described by the following diagram:

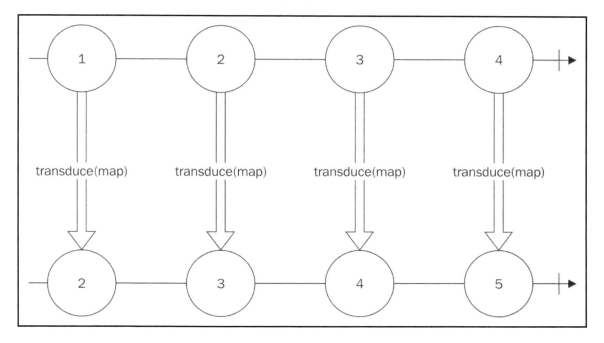

Notice that the transducer passed as an argument to the transduce operator is the same transducer used to apply transformations in an array in the previous section; we can even use the same transducer in two different objects, as can be seen in the following code:

```
var mapTransducer = t.map((i)=>i+1);

Rx.Observable
  .of(1,2,3,4)
  .transduce(mapTransducer)
  .subscribe((i)=>console.log(i));

var resultArray = t.into(
  [],
  mapTransducer,
  [1,2,3,4]
);
console.log(resultArray);
```

In this code we basically added a code to run the same `mapTransducer` used in the observable sequence over an array, and the output is as follows:

```
2
3
4
5
[ 2, 3, 4, 5 ]
```

As expected, the values of the observable sequence are printed one by one, containing the original values plus 1 and the array sequence is also printed containing the original values of the array plus 1, without any error. This shows the versatility of transducers as they can be used in different data structures without any change.

We can also use composition with transducers in RxJS, using the following code:

```
var mapTransducer = t.map((i)=>i+1);
var filterTransducer = t.filter((i)=>i%2===0);
var composedTransducer = t.comp(mapTransducer,filterTransducer);

Rx.Observable
  .of(1,2,3,4)
  .transduce(composedTransducer)
  .subscribe((i)=>console.log(i));
```

As you can see, the transducer is composed in exactly the same way as it was in the array examples, and we use the `composedTransducer` on the `transduce()` operator to run it over the observable.

The execution of this code gives us the following output:

```
2
4
```

The following code can be described by the following diagram:

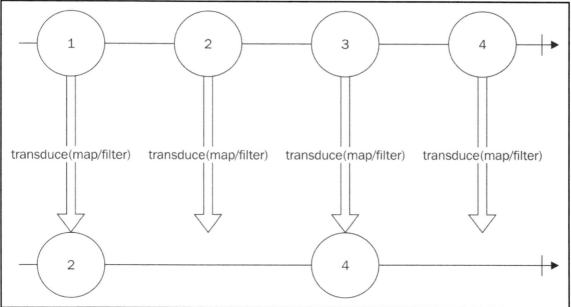

As you can see in the diagram, no intermediate observable is created; the same code can be implemented using the map() and filter() operators of observables, but it would add the creation of an extra observable, decreasing your code performance.

If we decided to implement the same code using the operators map() and filter() instead of a transducer, we could use the following code:

```
var mapFunction = (i)=>i+1;
var filterFunction = (i)=>i%2===0;

Rx.Observable
  .of(1,2,3,4)
  .map(mapFunction)
  .filter(filterFunction)
  .subscribe((i)=>console.log(i));
```

The output of this code would be the same, but under the hood it creates intermediate observables, as can be seen in this diagram:

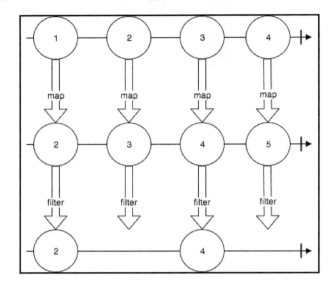

Testing transducers

When using transducers you can decouple the logic to transform your data from the source of your data; this way you can create tests for each one of your transducers without having to add an observable.

To test transducers we will use the exact same tools we used to test observables so far; the difference is that we can test the logic of the transducers using any iterable source of data such as an array or an observable.

Since observables are asynchronous data structure by nature, every time we want to test an observable, or to test the transformations applied to an observable, we need to create asynchronous tests. As transducers work independently of the current source of data we can use arrays to its behavior; using arrays we can create synchronous tests, which usually make them faster and easier to write and read.

Let's see how we can use an observable to test a transducer. To do so, let's first create a transducer to map a number to it plus 1 and then filter to keep only even numbers; this is the same transducer we already use in previous examples, so there is no need to explain each step:

```
var mapAndFilter = t.comp(
  t.map((i)=>i+1),
  t.filter((i)=>i%2===0)
);
```

Now we can create a unit test for it using an observable:

```
var assert = require('assert');

describe('Transducer test', function() {
  it('should return empty when running for empty observables',
function(done) {
    var found = false;
    Rx.Observable.empty()
      .transduce(mapAndFilter)
      .subscribe(
      function(){
        found = true;
      },
      function noop(){},
      function(){
        assert.equal(false,found);
        done();
      }
    );
  });
});
```

So far, we have only one test; this test checks if the transducer returns empty if the source of data is empty. To implement this, we first create a flag variable called `found`; this flag will be turned to true is we propagate any content in this observable. We add an `empty()` function to our error listener, and we check if our flag is still false and then finish the test when we complete the observable.

If the `found` flag still has the value `false`, this means that no element was propagated. If we run this test we will see the following message in the console, showing that our test passed:

```
[bash-3.2$ mocha example9_7_test.js


  Transducer test
    ✓ should return empty when running for empty observables


  1 passing (10ms)
```

Let's add one more test using an observable containing some values:

```
it('should return propagates 2,4 when running for an observable containing
1,2,3,4', function(done) {
    Rx.Observable.of(1,2,3,4)
      .transduce(mapAndFilter)
      .toArray()
      .subscribe(
        function(value){
          assert.equal(2,value.length);
          assert.equal(2,value[0]);
          assert.equal(4,value[1]);
        },
        function noop(){},
        function(){
          done();
        }
      );
});
```

In this new test we add a test case using an observable containing the values 1, 2, 3, and 4, we then apply the transducer to it and the operator `toArray()` on the result observable to create a new observable that propagates only one array containing all the values from this observable. We know the propagated value must be the array [2, 4], and to check this we must add three assertions; the first ensures that we have an array with two elements, the second ensures that the first element is 2, and the third ensures that the second element is 4. We finally finish the test when the observable completes.

If we run this test we will see the following message in the console, showing that our test passed:

```
[bash-3.2$ mocha example9_7_test.js


Transducer test
  ✓ should return empty when running for empty observables
  ✓ should return propagates 2,4 when running for an observable containing 1,2,3,4


2 passing (13ms)
```

But we all know that transducers can run independently of the data source, so we can create the exact same tests more easily using a synchronous approach via arrays instead of observables. Let's add two more tests to our `suite` using arrays instead of observable sequences:

```javascript
it('should return empty when running for empty data sources',function(){
    var dataSource = [];
    var result = t.into(
      [],
      mapAndFilter,
      dataSource
    );
    assert.equal(0,result.length);
});
it('should propagates 2,4 when running for a data source containing
1,2,3,4',function(){
    var dataSource = [1,2,3,4];
    var result = t.into(
      [],
      mapAndFilter,
      dataSource
    );
    assert.equal(2,result.length);
    assert.equal(2,result[0]);
    assert.equal(4,result[1]);
});
```

The tests with arrays instead of observables are a lot easier to understand given their synchronous nature. On the first, we create an empty array, apply the transducer to it, and check if the result is empty, while in the second we create an array containing the elements we want to test and do three assertions to ensure that it returns the expected result. If we run our test `suite` with our new test cases we will see the following output in our console:

```
[bash-3.2$ mocha example9_7_test.js


Transducer test
    ✓ should return empty when running for empty observables
    ✓ should propagates 2,4 when running for an observable containing 1,2,3,4
    ✓ should return empty when running for empty data sources
    ✓ should propagates 2,4 when running for a data source containing 1,2,3,4


4 passing (15ms)
```

It shows that all tests have passed, as we expected.

With transducers we can easily test the transformations we want to apply in our data, and it is even easier as we can use synchronous data structures to test, such as arrays, instead of asynchronous ones, such as observables.

A performance comparison for JavaScript code using transducers

One of the advantages of using transducers with RxJS is the performance improvement you can get from this, so far we have just commented on this improvement, now we will add some benchmarks so you can see the performance benefits for yourself. The results presented here are based on running on my personal computer; executions on different computers might lead to different results.

The most used and famous library for running benchmarks is called `benchmarks`. We can install it to run in Node.js environments using `npm`. To add it to your project just type the following command:

```
npm install benchmark@2.1.2
```

Before we start to use the library to benchmark transducers, let's see how we can use it through an example. Let's compare the difference between calling a function to sum two numbers using `call` or `apply`:

```
var Benchmark = require('benchmark')
var suite = new Benchmark.Suite;

var sum = (a,b)=>a+b;

suite.add('Sum using call', function() {
  sum.call(this,1,2);
})
.add('Sum using apply', function() {
  sum.apply(this,[1,2]);
})
.on('cycle', function(event) {
  console.log(event.target.toString());
})
.on('complete', function() {
  console.log('Fastest is ' + this.filter('fastest').map('name'));
})
.run();
```

In our example, we do the following steps:

1. Require the benchmark module.
2. Create a new `suite` of tests and store it in the `suite` variable.
3. Create the function we want to benchmark.
4. We must add functions to be tested in our `suite`; to do this we call the `add()` method, passing a string to identify this test, and the function to be tested. In the first test we want to see the performance of calling the `sum()` function using `call`.
5. The next test added to the `suite` runs the same function using apply.
6. We add a listener to the `cycle` event, which is called every time one cycle of benchmarks is finalized; we add a console log to show the performance results of this test.
7. We add a listener to the `complete` event, which is called when our test `suite` finishes; here we log the `fastest` test.
8. We run our performance test.

I named this file `benchmark_example_1.js`, so to run this performance test you must execute the following command:

```
node benchmark_example_1.js
```

When executing this program, it will take a few seconds before you see anything printed in the console; don't worry, `benchmark.js` is running the first test of our `suite`, and as soon as it is available it will print the results as follows:

```
[bash-3.2$ node benchmark_example_1.js
Sum using call x 56,758,714 ops/sec ±0.37% (94 runs sampled)
Sum using apply x 37,697,012 ops/sec ±0.84% (87 runs sampled)
Fastest is Sum using call
```

The first two lines show the execution of each test of our `suite`; the first number shows the number of operations it could do per second (higher is better), the second, the percentage, is the margin of error of this result, and the last is the number of samples it needed to execute to find this margin of error. The last line prints the `fastest` method, and it shows the `fastest` method is to use call instead of apply.

In our execution it was able to execute the sum using call `56,758,714` times per second with a margin of error of `0.37%`, and the test with apply `37,697,012` times per second with a margin of error of `0.84%`; as we can see, the ops/sec of `Sum using call` is higher and for this reason it is faster.

Now let's see the difference of when transducers instead of regular transformations on RxJS. We will benchmark the same transducer containing a simple `map()` and `filter()` function. So we first must create the functions used to map and filter along with the values we want to propagate in our observable:

```
var values = [1,2,3,4];
var mapFunction = (i)=>i+1;
var filterFunction = (i)=>i%2===0;
```

After this we must create the tests of our `suite`; the first test will be implemented using transducers:

```
suite.add('Transducer', function(deferred) {
  var transducer = t.comp(
    t.map(mapFunction),
    t.filter(filterFunction)
  );
  Rx.Observable.fromArray(values)
    .transduce(transducer)
    .subscribe(function(){}, function(){}, function(){
```

```
        deferred.resolve();
    });
},{defer:true})
```

We first create our transducer, then an observable using the array we created. And as this is an asynchronous test we call `deferred.resolve()` when our test is concluded and we add the flag `defer:true` to mark our test as an asynchronous test.

Now we need to create the test using regular `map()` and `filter()` operators; it can be done as follows:

```
.add('Map/Filter', function(deferred) {
   Rx.Observable.fromArray(values)
     .map(mapFunction)
     .filter(filterFunction)
     .subscribe(function(){},function(){},function(){
       deferred.resolve();
     });
},{defer:true})
```

After this we must add the listeners to log the results of our tests as we did in our first example:

```
on('cycle', function(event) {
   console.log(event.target.toString());
})
.on('complete', function() {
   console.log('Fastest is ' + this.filter('fastest').map('name'));
})
.run();
```

Then we can execute the code, and see the results:

```
[bash-3.2$ node benchmark_example_2.js
Transducer x 159,280 ops/sec ±1.25% (44 runs sampled)
Map/Filter x 148,195 ops/sec ±0.33% (44 runs sampled)
Fastest is Transducer
```

Looking at the results we can see the transducer is a little faster than the `map()`/`filter()` option, but let's see what happens if we change our array containing the values of the observables, so our observables propagate more data:

```
var values =
[1,2,3,4,5,6,7,8,9,10,11,12,13,14,15,16,17,18,19,20,21,22,23,24,25];
```

Now if were run our `suite` of tests we will see:

```
[bash-3.2$ node benchmark_example_2.js
Transducer x 50,562 ops/sec ±0.69% (41 runs sampled)
Map/Filter x 37,451 ops/sec ±0.44% (43 runs sampled)
Fastest is_Transducer
```

The number of operations per second is decreased in both, as is expected since we are processing more data. Perhaps the performance improvement from using transducers is a lot better, on our first execution the `map()`/`filter()` implementation was almost 7% slower than the transducer implementation, but in this execution it was almost *26%* slower, so it's clear that you can have great performance improvements using transducers on big observables.

Looking at the results we can see real performance gains with the use of transducers.

Summary

In this chapter, we learned what transducers are. They are a way to compose transformations to be applied to iterable sources, and they are independent of the data source.

We learned the advantages of using transducers–algorithmic transformation composition, performance improvement, better testability, better readability, and independency from the data source

In the advantages we learned how we can compose multiple transformations to create a transformation decoupled from the data source, and how we can reuse the same transducer in completely different data sources.

One section showed the advantage of testing a transducer, as it lets us use synchronous code to test, and how we can have a big performance improvement using this tool.

Now you are ready to create and implement your own applications using functional reactive programming; remember you had the advantage of using Reactive Extensions throughout this book, so most of the knowledge you learned here can be used in other platforms or languages as there are several implementations of Reactive Extensions on other platforms.

Functional reactive programming is an amazing way to model your application and to handle the flow of your data, and you have already mastered it. Congratulations.

Before we finish this book I felt that it was important to have a first hands-on with you on functional reactive programming, to do so I decided to create a web chat project using it. Web chat is a perfect candidate for functional reactive programming as it implies a continuous source of data flowing to and from your application.

In the next chapter, we will implement the server side of our web chat application, using nodes; we will go through the implementation and test of our code, so we will see how we can model our messages and listen to incoming messages from the client, and also how we can better deliver them.

I expect to use most of the concepts that we have learned in this book in the next two chapters, so let's create our first project.

10
A Real-Time Server

In the last chapter, we covered an advanced topic in functional reactive programming, called the transducer. Transducers enable us to create a composition of transformations of data. One of the main advantages of transducers is the possibility of making your data transformations independent from the source of your data; with the `transducers-js` library we can use transducers on observables and in any iterable object.

With transducers, we can:

- Write better tests as it make it easy to decouple the source of the data to the transformations applied to it
- Improve the performance of our code; as it skips the need for any intermediate iterable
- Improve the maintainability of your code, when we compose transformations to create new transformations we can reuse them throughout our codebase, and avoiding code repetition is a good idea

Throughout this book, we have learned:

- What are observables?
- What is an operator?
- How can we listen to incoming data?
- How can we transform incoming data?
- How can we compose different sources of data?
- How can we reuse sources of data?
- How can we mitigate the problem of receiving data faster than we can process?
- Two different frameworks to implement functional reactive programming in JavaScript

- How can we test programs using RxJS?
- What is a transducer?

With all this knowledge, you should feel capable of implementing your own application using functional reactive programming, but before you start a new application, I wanted to give you an example application using extensively functional reactive programming on both server and client.

Our example application will consist of a client application to run in the browser and a server application to run on the node. On both I will show you the architecture of the application and the reasons to choose this architecture, along with code and tests for this code.

A web chat is the perfect application to show the use of observables and RxJS as this is a highly interactive application. To create it we will use a **WebSocket server** to receive and deliver user messages.

In this chapter, we will explore the following topics:

- Implement a WebSocket-based server in JavaScript
- Use observables to listen and deliver data to the web chat application clients
- Create tests for our application
- See how we could scale our application if needed, making it support a publish/subscriber server as Redis, to receive and deliver message to other servers

The web chat server

To show the use of functional reactive programming and RxJS in JavaScript projects we will implement a web chat server. This is a perfect choice, because of the nature of this application.

In web chats users are constantly sending and receiving message; on some implementations of chat servers you can even send commands to remove or block a user, set reminders, and other things right from the text box. So, it is really easy to see how messages can be modeled as data being propagated through an observable sequence and how it is important to distinguish messages coming from this channel (commands from user messages).

There is also the possibility of implementing this server using WebSocket, which will also show us how RxJS is a perfect fit for any application using WebSockets.

Last but not least, it is important to notice that a web chat application can be easy to implement, but it can become arbitrarily complex as you decide to create new features for it.

For our web chat application, the idea is to keep it simple, but show you how you could implement more complex features. Our web chat application will have:

- Broadcast messages
- Private messages
- Some commands
- Tests

 Some features are common on chat applications, such as channels/rooms, but we will not implement these as you can implement them easily just deriving each from the implemented features. We also will not implement logins and passwords for users as it is completely beyond the scope of this book and would not give you any additional knowledge.

Creating the project

We will implement the backend of our web chat application in the node, so the first thing is to create a folder to store our project and, inside this folder, start the project using the following command:

```
npm init
```

This command will ask you for a lot of metadata for the project. You can leave all the defaults in force, just hitting *Enter* until the end. After this we need to install some libraries we will use to implement our project; the first one is RxJS, and to install it you must type the following command:

```
npm install rx@4.1.0 --save
```

We also need a library to implement our WebSocket server: we will use the most famous library to implement WebSocket in JavaScript socket.io with the following command:

```
npm install socket.io@1.7.3 --save
```

We will use express to serve the HTML page of our client, so we need to install it:

```
npm install --save express@4.15.2
```

Lastly, we need a runner to execute the tests of our application, and for this we will install `mocha` with the following command:

```
npm install mocha@3.2.0 -save-dev
```

Inside your project folder, you should create two new folders: one called `src` where we will place the source code of our application, and the other called `tests` where we will place all the tests of our application.

After this initial step, you should have your project folder containing a file called `package.json`, and three folders named `node_modules`, `src`, and `tests`.

 You can choose different names for your folders containing the source and tests, but this will be the name used in this book so, if you do change them, remember to change names when executing certain commands.

The architecture of the server

To implement the features we described before, we will use a simple architecture, and we will need only three files on our source code.

The first one is the `index.js` file containing the initialization of our WebSocket server and receiving the messages from the chat users; the data from each user will be implemented as an observable. All data passed through this observable will call the service responsible for that message, and the attribute `service` of each message will contain the name of the service.

All services are going to be implemented in a single file, called `services.js`; each service in this file might return an observable and, in the case of an observable being returned, our client will start to listen to messages from that observable. Initially we will have only four services:

- `sendMessage()`: This service sends message to the connected clients; it can be a private message or a broadcast message. The attribute of the message will contain the receiver of that message.
- `listenToMessages()`: This service returns an observable containing all messages directed to that client.
- `blockUser()`: This service returns an observable without the messages from the blocked user.

- command(): This service can be used to implement some commands. We will initially implement only two commands, one to show the current time to all users, and the other to echo your own messages. Using this method you can easily create new commands.

Finally, the last part of your project is our data source, called data_source.js. For our first implementation, there is no reason to save or retrieve data to a database, as this is just a sample application and we do not want to keep a history of messages or any other features that need a database. So, our data source will consist of only one observable (actually a subject) where we can push and listen to data.

If we needed to keep a history we could easily add a MongoDB, or any other database, to our application to retrieve this message history.

After our initial implementation, we will add a Redis server to use it to communicate messages through our servers.

This diagram describes how communication works on our server:

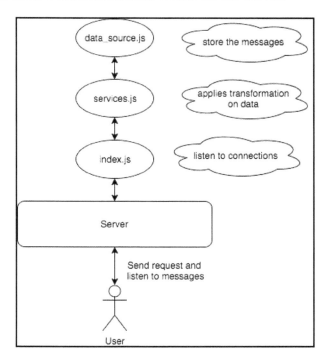

Implementing the server

To implement our server, we need to implement the three parts of our system described in the previous example. We will first create our data source, then our WebSocket server, and finally our services and their tests.

DataSource

As we have no interest in keep the history of messages nor in implementing a login for our server (the users are going to just type a name and this name will be used), we can use a simple observable to implement our DataSource; this DataSource will contain only the messages sent from user to user and broadcast messages.

Our DataSource must have two methods: the first to push new messages, and the second to listen to incoming messages. We can use a RxJS Subject to implement this behavior as it lets us push data to our observable. We could also user an observable using the create() method to create it from an arbitrary source, but the code with a Subject will be a lot easier to read and to understand:

```
let Rx = require('rx');
let messagesSubject = new Rx.Subject();
module.exports = {
  push(data){
    messagesSubject.onNext(data);
  },
  get(){
    return messagesSubject;
  }
};
```

In this code, we executed the following steps:

1. Created a Subject and stored it in the messagesSubject variable.
2. Exported an object containing two methods:
    - The first method is the push() method, which only calls the onNext() method of this Subject with the provided data to push it through the Subject
    - The second method is the get() method, which only returns our Subject so others can listen to data

On our data source we could have just instantiated our `Subject` and exported it, but it would couple our data source to an RxJS implementation, and every file requiring it would have to know it needed to use the method `onNext()` to push data. This is not a problem now, as this is just an example application, but it will be a problem as soon as we add Redis (or any other database), and for this reason I decided to create this object instead of just exporting the `Subject` object.

 I will not create tests for our data source for the same reason: we can easily create tests for it now, but as soon as we add any database to it, you would probably have to find a way to mock that database if you wanted to continue to test your data source, and this goes beyond the scope of this book.

Service to send messages

The first service we will create is the service to send messages. This message can be sent to a single user (private) or to all users (broadcast).

Our service will have the following signature:

```
sendMessage(payload);
```

This service does not have a return, and it receives only one parameter which is mandatory:

- `payload`: This is an object containing the message to be sent; it must have up to three properties:
    - `from`: This property is mandatory, it is a string representing the user sending the message
    - `content`: This property is mandatory, it is a string representing the content of the message
    - `to`: This property is optional, it is a string representing the receiver of the message; if it is omitted, the message is sent to all users

Our service must implement the following rules:

- Must support sending a message to all users (broadcast)
- Must support sending a message to a single user (private)
- Cannot send a message if the payload is not provided
- Cannot send a message without content (content property) or without a sender (from property)

Before we implement our service, we need to create a test for it.

Test implementation

In the previous section we created our DataSource and, so far, our DataSource consists of just an RxJS subject where we can push and listen to data. However, our data source could be a database, and for this reason for our tests we will always use a mock DataSource. So, let's implement our mock DataSource; inside the `tests` folder create a file called `mock_datasource_factory.js`, and paste in the following code:

```
let Rx = require('rx');
module.exports = function(){
    let messagesSubjectMock = new Rx.Subject();
    return{
        push(data){
            messagesSubjectMock.onNext(data);
        },
        get(){
            return messagesSubjectMock;
        }
    };
};
```

In this code we export a function that, when executed, creates a `Subject` and returns an object containing the methods `push()` and `get()` to send data and to listen to data. Our implementation looks a lot like the original DataSource implementation, but as we create a new `Subject` on every function call, we can execute it in each test so each one has its own DataSource. This way a test cannot impact on another test.

Now, let's implement our tests; for this service we need to implement only two tests: one to check if the method can send private messages, and the other to check if it can send broadcast messages. A more complete suite would also implement checks to see if the service enforces the `payload` to not be null, and if it contains the `from` and `content` property, but it would make our code bigger and harder to keep within the confines of a book, so let's just keep our test simple.

Before we implement our tests, we must create at least a dummy implementation of our services so we can test it: in the `src` folder create a file called `services.js` and paste in the following code:

```
module.exports = function(dataSource){
  return{
    sendMessage(){},
    command(){},
```

```
      listenToMessages(){},
      blockUser(){}
    };
};
```

Our file will export a function that receives a `datasource` as an argument and returns an object containing our four methods. We implement it this way so that we can inject a `datasource` in our services, and so that we can run our tests with a DataSource and our application with a different one.

Now that we have the basic structure, let's implement our tests: on the tests folder create a file called `send_message_test.js` and paste in the following code:

```
let assert = require('assert');
let mockDataSourceFactory = require('./mock_datasource_factory');
let servicesFactory = require('../src/services');
```

Here we just require the `assert` module to do our tests assertions, our module to create a mock DataSource, and our module to create the `services`. Now add the test suite with a single test:

```
describe('Send Message Test',function(){
    it('Must support sending a message',function(done){
        let mockDataSource = mockDataSourceFactory();
        let services = servicesFactory(mockDataSource);
        let from = 'Jim';
        let to = 'John Doe';
        let content = 'foobar';
        let message = {to:to,content:content, from:from};
        let subscription = mockDataSource
                .get()
                .subscribe(function(message){
                        assert.equal(message.from,from);
                        assert.equal(message.to,to);
                        assert.equal(message.content,content);
                        subscription.dispose();
                        done();
                });
        services.sendMessage(message);

    });
});
```

Here we created our test suite to test the `sendMessage` service. We also added a test to our suite using the `it()` function. This test will check if our service can send data to a user. On the service implementation we first create a DataSource (`mockDataSource`); on the next line we create services using this DataSource and store them in the `services` variable (we will do it in every test); then we create a sender for our message (`from`), the receiver (`to`) and the content (`content`); and, finally, we create our message (`message`). The next thing to do is to listen to our mock DataSource to see if the message was sent. We add a subscription to it and, in this subscription, we verify the message properties (`from`, `to`, and `content`). Then we finish our subscription and call the `done()` method to finish our test. The last step is to send the message.

With this test done, we can implement the next test to verify whether our service can send messages to all users, so add the following test to our test suite:

```
it('Must support broadcast message',function(done){
        let mockDataSource = mockDataSourceFactory();
        let services = servicesFactory(mockDataSource);
        let from = 'Jim';
        let content = 'foobar';
        let message = {content:content, from:from};
        let subscription = mockDataSource
                .get()
                .subscribe(function(message){
                        assert.equal(message.from,from);
                        assert.equal(message.content,content);
                        subscription.dispose();
                        done();
                });
        services.sendMessage(message);
});
```

The test is similar to the test for private messages. We only omitted the property `to` from the message, as messages without a receiver must be sent to all users.

Now we can run our test suite against our services. To do this run the following command inside your projects folder:

```
mocha tests/send_message_test.js
```

After running this test, we can see the result in the console:

```
[bash-3.2$ mocha tests/send_message_test.js


  Send Message Test
    1) Must support sending a message
    2) Must support broadcast message


  0 passing (4s)
  2 failing

  1) Send Message Test Must support sending a message:
     Error: timeout of 2000ms exceeded. Ensure the done() callback is being called in this test.

  2) Send Message Test Must support broadcast message:
     Error: timeout of 2000ms exceeded. Ensure the done() callback is being called in this test.
```

As you can see, all our tests failed as we do not have an implementation for our service yet.

Service implementation

Now that we have the test for our service we are ready to create the implementation of this service. To do this, change the current implementation of the sendMessage service in the services.js file to the following:

```
sendMessage(payload){
    if(payload && payload.content && payload.from){
      dataSource.push({
        from: payload.from,
        to:payload.to,
        content: payload.content
      });
    }
  }
```

The implementation of our service is simple: it just verifies whether the payload exists and whether it has content and from properties; if our argument is valid all we have to do is to push the message to our datasource.

Now we can run our test again using the same command and see the results:

```
[bash-3.2$ mocha tests/send_message_test.js


Send Message Test
   ✓ Must support sending a message
   ✓ Must support broadcast message



2 passing (11ms)
```

Now our services are passing as expected, so we can go to the next service.

Service to listen to new messages

Our next service will be used to listen to new messages. It must return an observable containing the data, the destination of which is the given user.

Our service will have the following signature:

```
listenToMessages(payload, [observable]);
```

It receives two parameters, but only the first is mandatory:

- `payload`: It is an object containing information about the user, and it must have one property:
    - `me`: This property is mandatory - it is a string representing the user listening to messages
- `observable`: It is the observable where messages are pushed

Our service must implement the following rules:

- Must return an observable containing only data for the given user, which means messages sent by the given user, private messages for that user, and broadcast messages
- If an observable is provided, we must change this observable to follow the first rule, and must apply the first rule to the DataSource (which contains all messages)

Now we know the rules, we can implement tests for them.

Test implementation

We are going to create three tests for this service: the first checks if the observable returned by this service contains data sent to the given user; the second checks if it contains broadcast messages; and the third checks that it does not contain private messages to other users.

Create a file called `listen_to_messages_test.js` and paste in the following code to create our test suite:

```
let assert = require('assert');
let mockDataSourceFactory = require('./mock_datasource_factory');
let servicesFactory = require('../src/services');

describe('Listen to message Test',function(){
    it('Must listen to messages sent to me',function(done){
        let mockDataSource = mockDataSourceFactory();
        let services = servicesFactory(mockDataSource);
        let me = 'John Doe';
        let content = 'foobar';
        let message = {to:me,content:content};
        let subscription = services
                .listenToMessages({me:me})
                .subscribe(function(message){
                        assert.equal(message.to,me);
                        assert.equal(message.content,content);
                        subscription.dispose();
                        done();
                });
        mockDataSource.push(message);
    });
});
```

The first test checks if the observable returned by the `sendMessage`service contains messages for the given user. This test is similar to the test for the `sendMessage` service, but here we are doing the opposite. We subscribe to the observable returned by the `listenToMessages()` service and directly push data to our mock DataSource on the last line of our test.

The next test will check if it contains a broadcast message:

```
it('Must listen to messages sent to all',function(done){
        let mockDataSource = mockDataSourceFactory();
        let services = servicesFactory(mockDataSource);
        let me = 'John Doe';
        let content = 'foobar';
        let message = {content:content};
```

```
    let subscription = services
            .listenToMessages({me:me})
            .subscribe(function(message){
                    assert.equal(message.content,content);
                    subscription.dispose();
                    done();
            });
        mockDataSource.push(message);
});
```

It is almost identical to the previous test. The only difference is that the message pushed into the DataSource does not contain a to property, which means a broadcast message.

In the last test we check that it does not contains private messages for other users:

```
it('Must not listen to messages sent to others',function(done){
        let mockDataSource = mockDataSourceFactory();
        let services = servicesFactory(mockDataSource);
        let receivedMessage = false;
        let me = 'John Doe';
        let to = 'other';
        let content = 'foobar';
        let message = {to:to,content:content};
        let subscription = services
                .listenToMessages({me:me})
                .subscribe(function(message){
                        receivedMessage = true;
                },function noop(){
                },function(){
                    assert.equal(receivedMessage,false);
                    done();
                });
        mockDataSource.push(message);
        mockDataSource.get().onCompleted();
});
```

Here our test is a little bit different: we push a message containing a to property, which is different from the user listening to the data, to check if we did not receive this message. We add a flag to the beginning of our test (receivedMessage) initializing it with false, on our subscription. If we receive any data we turn our flag to true. We put an empty function to listen for errors, and add a function to be called when the observable completes. This function checks whether our flag is still false and ends our test. After creating our subscription, we must push the message and finish the observables.

Now we have our three tests implemented, and we can execute them using the command:

```
mocha tests/listen_to_messages_test.js
```

The results are in the console:

This shows all our tests failed, as expected.

Service implementation

All we have to do now is to implement our service. To do this, change the
`listenToMessages()` service in the file `services.js` to use this implementation:

```
listenToMessages(payload, observable){
    let me = payload.me;
    observable = observable || dataSource.get();
    return observable.filter(function(message){
        return !message.to || message.to === me || message.from === me;
    });
}
```

Our service is simple: on the first line we store the user, on the next line we store the
`observable` we will listen to; if no `observable` is provided we get the `observable` from
the DataSource containing all messages,; we then return the `observable` resulting from
applying a filter to check that the message does not have a `to` property (broadcast), or if the
`to` property is equal to the user (private), or if the `from` property is equal to the user (the
message sent by the user).

When we run the test again, we will see, in our console, that all the tests pass:

```
[bash-3.2$ mocha tests/listen_to_messages_test.js

  Listen to message Test
    ✓ Must listen to messages sent to me
    ✓ Must listen to messages sent to all
    ✓ Must not listen to messages sent to others


  3 passing (12ms)
```

Now our tests are passing, so we are one step closer to our web chat server.

 With these two services, we already have all the services we need for a very basic web chat, and we will add two more services to enhance our skills.

Service to block messages from a given user

The next service will be used to block messages from a given user. It must return an observable, and this observable cannot propagate messages sent by the blocked user.

Our service will have the following signature:

```
blockUser(payload, [observable]);
```

It receives two parameters, but only the first is mandatory:

- payload: This is an object containing information about the user to be blocked; it must have two properties:
    - me: This property is mandatory, it is a string representing the user listening to messages
    - blocked: This property is mandatory, it is a string representing the user to be blocked
- observable: The observable where messages for this user are pushed

Our service must implement the following rules:

- Must return an observable, and this observable cannot contain any message sent by the blocked user
- If no observable is provided, it must call the `listenToMessages()` service to get the observable of that user

Now we know the rules we can implement a test.

Test implementation

We will create only one test for our `blockUser()` service: our test will check that we do not receive messages from a given user after calling the service.

Create a file called `block_user_test.js` and paste in the following code to implement our test suite:

```
let assert = require('assert');
let mockDataSourceFactory = require('./mock_datasource_factory');
let servicesFactory = require('../src/services');

describe('Block user Test',function(){
    it('Must not receive message from blocked user',function(done){
        let mockDataSource = mockDataSourceFactory();
        let services = servicesFactory(mockDataSource);
        let receivedMessage = false;
        let me = 'John Doe';
        let blocked = 'Jim';
        let content = 'foobar';
        let message = {to:me,content:content};
        let subscription = services
                .blockUser({blocked:blocked,me:me})
                .subscribe(function(message){
                        receivedMessage = true;
                },function noop(){
                },function(){
                    assert.equal(receivedMessage,true);
                    subscription.dispose();
                    done();
                });
        mockDataSource.push(message);
        mockDataSource.get().onCompleted();
    });
});
```

In our test, we create a message to be sent to a user, we then use the `blockUser()` service to block messages from that user, and subscribe to the returned observable. We implement the same trick from the last test of the `listenToMessages()` service test using a flag to ensure we do not receive the message.

We can run this test with the following command:

```
mocha tests/block_user_test.js
```

When we run this code, we will see the following printed in our console:

```
[bash-3.2$ mocha tests/block_user_test.js


  Block user Test
    1) Must not receive message from blocked user


  0 passing (10ms)
  1 failing

  1) Block user Test Must not receive message from blocked user:
      TypeError: Cannot read property 'subscribe' of undefined
        at Context.<anonymous> (tests/block_user_test.js:14:71)
```

Again, our test failed as expected as we have not implemented our service yet.

Service implementation

Now its time to implement our service to block messages from a given user. To do this, change the `blockUser()` service in the file `services.js` to use this implementation:

```
blockUser(payload, observable) {
    let blocked = payload.blocked;
    observable = observable || this.listenToMessages(payload);
    return observable.filter(function(message) {
      return message.from !== blocked;
    });
  }
```

The implementation is similar to that from the `listenToMessages()` service. We have to call the filter operator to avoid propagating messages from the blocked user. One important thing is, if an observable is not passed as an argument, we get one from the `listenToMessages()` service, as it ensures a user listens only to messages he can listen to.

If we run our tests against this implementation, we will see this result in the console:

```
[bash-3.2$ mocha tests/block_user_test.js


  Block user Test
    ✓ Must not receive message from blocked user


  1 passing (11ms)
```

This test is now passing, so we need to implement just one last service.

Service to send a command

The last service we will implement will be a service to execute a command. On several web chats you can pass commands using the slash (/) character at the beginning of the message. Each web chat has its own implementation, and they can perform different actions such as kick another user, ban a user, send a GIF for every user, show the current time, and so on.

In our service to send a command, we will implement two different and simple commands: the first command will generate a random number between 1 and 6 and will be called `roll_a_dice`; the other command will be called `echo` and it will just send back the message sent by the user.

Our service will have the following signature:

```
command(payload);
```

It will receive only one mandatory parameter:

- `payload`: This is an object containing information to execute a command; it can have up to three properties:
    - `from`: This property is mandatory; it is a string representing the user sending the command.
    - `action`: This property is mandatory; it is a string representing the command (in our implementation it can be `roll_a_dice` or `echo`).
    - `content`: This property is used only by the `echo` command; it contains the string to be echoed back to the user

Our service must implement the following rules:

- Must implement the `roll_a_dice` command, which is sent back to the user executing the command, a message containing a random number between 1 and 6
- Must implement the `echo` command, which is sent back to the user executing the command, message equal to that sent by the user
- All messages sent by this service must have the server as sender of the message
- If case a user calls the command service passing a command that is not supported, the server must respond to the user informing him this command is not supported

Now we know the rules we can implement tests for them.

Test implementation

We will create three tests for our command service: the first will test if the `roll_a_dice` command works as expected; the second will check the `echo` command; and the last will check the response of the service when using a command that is not supported.

Create a file called `command_test.js` and paste in the following code to implement our test suite:

```
let assert = require('assert');
let mockDataSourceFactory = require('./mock_datasource_factory');
let servicesFactory = require('../src/services');

describe('Command Test',function(){
    it('Must support roll_a_dice command',function(done){
        let mockDataSource = mockDataSourceFactory();
```

```
        let services = servicesFactory(mockDataSource);
        let me = 'John Doe';
        let message = {from:me,action:'roll_a_dice'};
        let myMessagesObservable = services.listenToMessages({me:me});
        let subscription = myMessagesObservable
                .subscribe(function(message){
                        assert.equal(message.from,'server');
                        assert.equal(message.to,me);
                        assert.equal(/Result is [1-6]/
                        .test(message.content),true);
                        subscription.dispose();
                        done();
                });
        services.command(message);
    });
});
```

Our first test will check if the `roll_a_dice` command works as expected. We first create our mock DataSource and generate our services as we did in the other tests. We then create an object containing a property `from` (the user using the command) and a property `action` equal to `roll_a_dice`, and store a variable called `message`. After this, we call the service to listen to messages to get our observable and subscribe to it. In our subscription we will check if the message sender is the server, if the receiver is the user that called the command, and if the content of the message is as expected. We finally call the command service to test it.

The next test will check whether the `echo` command works as expected:

```
it('Must support echo command',function(done){
        let mockDataSource = mockDataSourceFactory();
        let services = servicesFactory(mockDataSource);
        let me = 'John Doe';
        let content= 'foobar';
        let message = {from:me,action:'echo',content:content};
        let myMessagesObservable = services.listenToMessages({me:me});
        let subscription = myMessagesObservable
                .subscribe(function(message){
                        assert.equal(message.from, 'server');
                        assert.equal(message.to,me);
                        assert.equal(message.content,content);
                        subscription.dispose();
                        done();
                });
        services.command(message);
    });
```

This service looks a lot like the other service. The only differences are that we change the action to echo, add a content property, and, on our subscription, we check if the content is the expected.

Our last test will assert what must happen when we execute a command that is not supported:

```
it('Must send a message if the action is not supported',function(done){
        let mockDataSource = mockDataSourceFactory();
        let services = servicesFactory(mockDataSource);
        let me = 'John Doe';
        let content= 'foobar';
        let message = {from:me,action:'some_action'};
        let myMessagesObservable = services.listenToMessages({me:me});
        let subscription = myMessagesObservable
                .subscribe(function(message){
                    assert.equal(message.from,'server');
                    assert.equal(message.to,me);
                    assert.equal(message.content,
                    'The action some_action is not supported');
                    subscription.dispose();
                    done();
                });
        services.command(message);
    });
```

Again, our test is similar to the others. The only differences are that we are changing the value of the action to a value not supported (some_action), and checking if the message replied by the service is the expected message.

To run our test, execute the following command:

```
mocha tests/command_test.js
```

When you run this command, you will see the test result in your console:

```
[bash-3.2$ mocha tests/command_test.js


  Command Test
    1) Must support roll_a_dice command
    2) Must support echo command
    3) Must send a message if the action is not supported


  0 passing (6s)
  3 failing

  1) Command Test Must support roll_a_dice command:
     Error: timeout of 2000ms exceeded. Ensure the done() callback is being called in this test.


  2) Command Test Must support echo command:
     Error: timeout of 2000ms exceeded. Ensure the done() callback is being called in this test.


  3) Command Test Must send a message if the action is not supported:
     Error: timeout of 2000ms exceeded. Ensure the done() callback is being called in this test.
```

All our services are failing, as expected.

Service implementation

To implement our `command` service, change your `services.js` file, switching the implementation of the `command` service to use this:

```
command(payload){
        switch(payload.action){
              case 'roll_a_dice':
                    this.sendMessage({
                            from:'server',
                            to:payload.from,
                            content:'Result is
                            '+Math.round(1+Math.random()*5)
                    });
                    break;
              case 'echo':
                    this.sendMessage({
                            from:'server',
                            to:payload.from,
                            content:payload.content
                    });
                    break;
              default:
```

```
this.sendMessage({
        from:'server',
        to:payload.from,
        content:'The action '+payload.action +' is not
        supported'});
    }
}
```

The implementation of our service is simple: we just use a switch block on the `action` property to decide which message we must send. The first case is `roll_a_dice`, in this case we send a message whose content is a message starting with `Result is` and containing a random number between 1 and 6.

The second case is for the `echo` command, where we just send a message containing the same content received.

If the `action` property does not satisfy any of the other cases, we go to the `default`, which only sends a message stating that the command is not supported.

Now we'll run our tests for this implementation:

```
[bash-3.2$ mocha tests/command_test.js


  Command Test
    ✓ Must support roll_a_dice command
    ✓ Must support echo command
    ✓ Must send a message if the action is not supported


  3 passing (13ms)
```

Our tests now pass, as expected.

This was the last service to implement. So, now that we have implemented all our services and tests, we can execute all our tests together with the following command:

```
mocha tests/*_test.js
```

We can see, in the console, that all our tests pass:

```
[bash-3.2$ mocha tests/*_test.js


  Block user Test
    ✓ Must not receive message from blocked user

  Command Test
    ✓ Must support roll_a_dice command
    ✓ Must support echo command
    ✓ Must send a message if the action is not supported

  Listen to message Test
    ✓ Must listen to messages sent to me
    ✓ Must listen to messages sent to all
    ✓ Must not listen to messages sent to others

  Send Message Test
    ✓ Must support sending a message
    ✓ Must support broadcast message


  9 passing (15ms)
```

Handling WebSocket connections

We will handle WebSocket connections using the `socket.io` library. This is the most used WebSocket library for the Node.js community.

Now, let's start our WebSocket implementation. Open your `index.js` file and put this code inside it:

```
let Rx = require('rx');
let dataSource = require('./data_source');
let services = require('./services')(dataSource);
```

For now, we've just imported reactive extensions, our DataSource, and created our `services`. Now we need to start the server:

```
let app = require('express')();
let http = require('http').Server(app);
let io = require('socket.io')(http);
http.listen(3000,()=>console.log('Server listening on port 3000'));
```

Here, we create an HTTP server, pass it to the `socket.io` library, and start it to listen on the port 3000. Now we have to wait for connections: to do this we create an `Observable` to listen to connection events:

```
Rx.Observable.fromEvent(io,'connection')
```

We create a subscription for it:

```
Rx.Observable.fromEvent(io,'connection')
  .subscribe(function(client) {
  });
```

Now we must implement the subscription, and on the subscription we must listen to events from that client. The client will send JSON as strings, so we need to parse it back to JSON. We also need to call the right service; every time our service returns a new `Observable`, we must switch to that `Observable`. Finally, we must stop our `Observable` when the client disconnects:

```
function(client) {
    let currentObservable = null;
    Rx.Observable.fromEvent(client, 'request')
        .map((payload)=>JSON.parse(payload))
        .flatMapLatest((payload)=> {
          let serviceObservable = services[payload.service](payload,
currentObservable);
          if(serviceObservable){
            currentObservable = serviceObservable;
          }
          return currentObservable;
        })
        .takeUntil(Rx.Observable.fromEvent(client,'disconnect'))
        .subscribe(data => client.emit('message',data));
    }
```

The first thing we need to do is to create a variable to store our current `Observable` being listened to; we need it because the `blockUser()` service must receive it as a parameter. Then we create an `Observable` for all events of the type `request` from our client, and map our payload into a JSON object using the `map()` operator.

Now we have an `Observable` which emits the JSON object sent by the client. The next step is to call the respective service. As we know our services might return an `Observable`, and in this case we must use it, we need to store it in the `currentObservable` variable; we use `flatMapLatest` instead of `flatMap`, because we want to keep only the last `Observable` returned.

We also must finish our `Observable` when the client disconnects, and we do this using the `takeUntil()` operator to finish the `Observable` if a client sends a disconnect event.

Finally, all we have to do is send the message back to our user, and we do this by adding a subscription in our observable.

So the following is the final code for our `index.js` file:

```
let Rx = require('rx');
let dataSource = require('./data_source');
let services = require('./services')(dataSource);
let app = require('express')();
let http = require('http').Server(app);
let io = require('socket.io')(http);
http.listen(3000, ()=>console.log('Server listening on port 3000'));

Rx.Observable.fromEvent(io, 'connection')
  .subscribe(function(client) {
    let observable = null;
    Rx.Observable.fromEvent(client, 'request')
      .map((payload)=>JSON.parse(payload))
      .flatMapLatest((payload)=> {
        let serviceObservable =
services[payload.service](payload,observable);
        if(serviceObservable){
          observable = serviceObservable;
        }
        return observable;
      })
      .takeUntil(Rx.Observable.fromEvent(client,'disconnect'))
      .subscribe(data => client.emit('message',data));
  });
```

That is all we need to implement a web chat using functional reactive programming with the RxJS library. In our implementation, everything is happening on the same server. Let's see how we can add more servers and make them communicate.

Scaling the server

Currently our implementation cannot be used if we decide to deploy several servers. Imagine the scenario where **user A** connects to **server A**, and **user B** connects to **server B**; **user A** and **user B** cannot chat, because they are on different servers.

To make users connected from different servers communicate, we need to find a way to make our server communicate, and we can do this using the Redis database. Among other amazing features, Redis supports what is called a publish/subscriber pattern. With this pattern, a server can publish a message, and all servers subscribed to listen to that message will receive it.

With this feature Redis is the perfect database to solve our problem of server communication, so let's see how we can connect to it to receive messages and also how we can change our data store to support it.

Connecting to Redis

To use Redis database we need a library to connect to it, the most common library for node is called ioredis. This library is available on npm and have support to all features of Redis.

To install `ioredis` just execute the following command in your project:

```
npm install ioredis@2.5.0 —save
```

As we discussed in the previous session, we will use Redis as a publish/subscriber broker for all messages in our web chat implementation.

Before start using Redis, you need to install it in your machine, you can follow the instructions in the official website on how to install it.

This diagram show what happens when a user send a message on an environment with multiple Node.js servers:

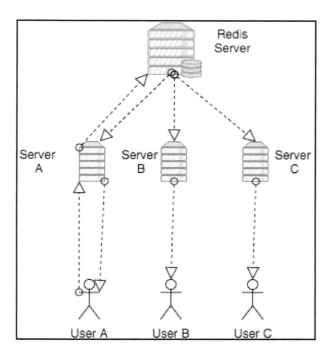

This diagram shows an user (named **User A**) which is connected to a server (named **Server A**), this user then sends a message to **Server A** , this server then publishes this message in Redis, all servers are subscribed to listen to messages on Redis Server, then Redis send the message to all servers each of them, finally sent back the message to all connected users.

This architecture is a simple implementation of how we could make several servers communicate, this is not intended to be the best architecture to solve this problem.

Using Redis as the DataSource for messages

Now we must change our DataSource to use Redis instead of the basic subject from our original implementation. To do so, just change the file data_source.js, to use this implementation instead:

```
let Rx = require('rx');
let Redis = require('ioredis');

let subscriber = new Redis();
let publisher = new Redis();
const TOPIC = 'web_chat';
subscriber.subscribe(TOPIC);
let messagesObservable =
Rx.Observable.fromEvent(subscriber, 'message', (channel,message)=>JSON.parse(
message));
module.exports = {
  push(data){
    publisher.publish(TOPIC,JSON.stringify(data));
  },
  get(){
    return messagesObservable;
  }
};
```

In this code we first import the RxJS and ioredis libraries; we then start two connections with the Redis server, one to publish and the other to listen to messages. As we are running Redis in a local machine, we do not need to pass any argument to the constructor. On the next line, we create a name for the TOPIC where the messages are going to be published. This name can be anything, but all servers must use the same TOPIC. You also don't need to manually create this TOPIC as Redis will create it for you automatically. We finally subscribe to this TOPIC and create an Observable to listen to messages from that subscription. The last thing we need to do is to implement the exported methods (push() and get()): on push() we only have to publish it to Redis and on get() we only have to return the created Observable.

This is all we need to do if we want to distribute our application across several servers using Redis to communicate between them.

Summary

In this chapter, we created our first application using RxJS. The `web chat` application is a perfect fit to use functional reactive programming given its interactive nature. In this chapter we learned to model a WebSocket server as an observable for connections using RxJS. We also learned to model our DataSource as an observable of messages, in two different flavors: firstly, keeping messages only on one local server and, secondly, sending messages to other servers using Redis as a publish/subscriber broker. We also looked at the use of operators to implement some of our services.

With this application, we saw how we can create observables from different event sources, and how we can use operators to implement some of our business rules.

Another important lesson from this chapter was the implementation of tests for our system. In our tests, we learned how to create a fake data source from a simple observable, and use a different one in each test to keep them independent from each other.

In the next chapter, we will implement the client side of our application. With this part of our application, we will see how we can model user interaction using functional reactive programming and an approach to implementing tests for functional reactive applications running inside the browser.

The next chapter will put to the test your ability to implement all the concepts you learned so far.

11
A Real-Time Client

In the last chapter, we implemented our first application using functional reactive programming; we decided to implement a real-time web chat using WebSockets because of its inherit nature of interactivity, making it a perfect candidate for functional reactive programming.

We decided to use RxJS in all levels of the application; we used it to:

- Model servers and incoming WebSocket connections
- Implement the business rule for some services
- Implement the DataSource of our application
- Implement the tests of our application

In our server implementation, we had the opportunity to implement observables from different sources and even implement a subject to push data.

From the tests perspective, we decided to implement some basic tests only for our services; we did not want to have full coverage of our code, but the constructs and architecture of these tests can be easily replicated to create more tests for our services or even to implement new tests for the other layers of our application.

Lastly, we learned how we can leverage Redis to communicate our servers application and we implemented a simple architecture to improve the scalability of our web chat. One important thing to notice, is how easy it was to introduce Redis to our application given the modular and decoupled architecture we used on our code.

This is the last chapter, and in this chapter, we will implement the client application for our real-time web chat; in this chapter you will learn:

- How to use RxJS in a client application
- How to model the messages received from the server through the WebSocket connection
- How to model inputs and the interactivity of users using functional reactive programming
- How to implement tests for client applications using RxJS
- Batch changes in the DOM to improve performance
- Package and build our application

For our web chat client we will not be using any **Single-Page Application** (**SPA**) framework; we will try to use the minimum number of libraries to implement our project. If you are using any specific framework, you can easily use the same constructs from this chapter in your personal projects.

Installing dependencies

To implement the client application for our web chat application, we will try to keep the dependencies to the minimum required; we are doing so to encourage you to avoid abusing the use of the library on your application and also to show how powerful a well structured application using RxJS for functional reactive programming can be.

To keep the code simple and avoid adding too many configurations, we are going to use **browserify** to bundle our client.

The browserify is a bundler that lets us use commonJS when implementing client-side applications. This means we can import data from different files/modules using require in the same way you do on Node.js applications.

To use `browserify` we must install it as a dependency in our application; to do this, we must run the following command on the folder of our application:

```
npm i browserify@14.1.0 --save-dev
```

With `browserify`, we can already bundle our application in a single JavaScript file.

We will not add a **minifier** for our JavaScript file, because this is just a sample application, but, when creating a real-life application, always minify your JavaScript file before sending it to your users.

To keep our application simple, we will also avoid using any CSS pre processor, and keep the style of the page to a minimum.

 You can use webpack or any other bundler on this application, and it is a good exercise for you to improve it at the end, making it as production-ready as it can be.

We will be using the same code base from the server application, so we do not need to install RxJS again as it was installed in the previous chapter. To implement our code, we will need only one more library, which is the `socket.io-client`.

We will use this client to connect using WebSocket and also send and receive messages from our server.

To install `socket.io-client` we must run the following code on the folder containing our application:

```
npm i socket.io-client@1.7.3 -save
```

Now that we have what we need to implement our application, we must install the dependencies that we will use to test our application.

The structure of our client

To implement our client application, we will create two folders in our project; the first is called `static` and it will contain the HTML page of our client and the built JavaScript file, the second will be called client and it will contain the JavaScript source code for our client application.

In the `static` folder, create a file called `index.html`, which will be the base HTML of our client, and paste the following code:

```
<!doctype html>
<html>
<head>
    <title>Reactive chat</title>
    <style>
        * { margin: 0; padding: 0; box-sizing: border-box; }
```

```
        body { font: 13px Helvetica, Arial; }
        .message_container { background: #ddd; padding: 3px; position:
fixed; bottom: 0; width: 100%; }
        .message_container input { border: 0; padding: 10px; width: 90%;
margin-right: .5%; }
        .message_container button { width: 9%; background: #99ff99; border:
none; padding: 10px; }
        #messages { list-style-type: none; margin: 0; padding: 0; }
        #messages li { padding: 5px 10px; }
        #messages li:nth-child(odd) { background: #eee; }
    </style>
</head>
<body>
<ul id="messages"></ul>
<div class="message_container">
    <input id="message_input"/><button id="send_message">Send
message</button>
</div>
<script src="/bundle.js"></script>
</body>
</html>
```

This HTML page contains only a minimum style to use in our chat, and also a `<ul>` element where we will show the chat messages, and a `<div>` containing one input where the user can enter messages, and also a button to send these messages. For the last, it uses a script file called `bundle.js`; this file will be created after our build process and will contain all the code we need to implement sample applications.

In the `client` folder we will need three files:

- `connection.js`: This file contains all the logic to connect to the WebSocket server; this logic includes sending and receiving messages from the server
- `events.js`: This file contains all the logic to listen to events from the DOM, so this file will map the user interaction into observable objects
- `index.js`: This file will make the connection between `connection.js` and `events.js`; in this file we will make the WebSocket connection listen to and receive messages from the DOM

So you already can create these files and keep them with an empty implementation.

After this you should have a folder structure like this one:

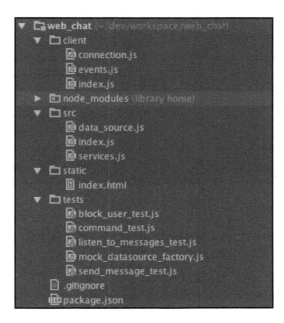

Now we are ready to build our application for the first time.

Building the application for the first time

To create our application, we must be able to serve at least two static files, the `index.html`, which is the HTML page, and the `bundle.js` file, which contains all the logic for the application written in JavaScript.

Serving the `static` file using `express` is extremely easy. To do so, let's change the `index.js` file inside the `src` folder (`src/index.js`) where we implemented our express server, and paste the following code:

```
app.use(express.static('static'));
```

This code tells express to serve all files in the `static` folder as static files; now we will be able to see our page for the first time. To do this, run your application with:

```
node src/index.js
```

Do not forget to start the Redis server as we are using it to communicate the messages. If you do not start your Redis server you will see an error like this:

```
Server listening on port 3000
[ioredis] Unhandled error event: Error: connect ECONNREFUSED 127.0.0.1:6379
    at Object.exports._errnoException (util.js:1007:11)
    at exports._exceptionWithHostPort (util.js:1030:20)
    at TCPConnectWrap.afterConnect [as oncomplete] (net.js:1080:14)
[ioredis] Unhandled error event: Error: connect ECONNREFUSED 127.0.0.1:6379
    at Object.exports._errnoException (util.js:1007:11)
    at exports._exceptionWithHostPort (util.js:1030:20)
    at TCPConnectWrap.afterConnect [as oncomplete] (net.js:1080:14)
[ioredis] Unhandled error event: Error: connect ECONNREFUSED 127.0.0.1:6379
    at Object.exports._errnoException (util.js:1007:11)
    at exports._exceptionWithHostPort (util.js:1030:20)
    at TCPConnectWrap.afterConnect [as oncomplete] (net.js:1080:14)
```

So, do not forget to run the Redis server.

After starting the Redis server, and running our node application, we can already see the `web chat` application on the browser for the first time, so enter `http://localhost:3000` into your browser and you will see the application running:

If you can see this screen, congratulations! We are one step closer to implementing our web chat application. Now that we are able to serve the static file for our application, we must find a way to build the JavaScript file; to do this we will need to use browserify.

The browserify receive as parameter a single file and will follow and add all the dependencies (require) of this file until it bundles everything in a single file. This file will contain all the code to run our web chat application. As we already installed browserify, all we have to do, is generate the file with the following command:

browserify client/index.js -o static/bundle.js

This command tells browserify to start with the index.js file in the client folder, and gather all dependencies to generate a file named bundle.js inside the static folder.

After running this code, you should see the generated bundle.js file inside the static folder.

 Now we are going to prepare our package.json file, so we will always test and build our application before starting it. Do not worry if you do not know exactly how to change the package.json file as I will paste the final result of it.

Let's modify our package.json file on the root of our project, to use it to build our application. First, let's add the tests for our server. As you probably remember–to test our server application, we must run the following command:

mocha tests/*test.js

So we must add this command to the test property, inside the scripts property in our package.json; now we can run our tests using the following command:

npm test

To run our project, we use the following command:

node src/index.js

So. we can add this command to the start property, inside the scripts property in the package.json file; now we can start our application using the following command:

npm start

Now let's add a command to build our client application on our `package.json`; let's add the `build-client` property, inside the `scripts` property in the `package.json` file containing the following command:

```
browserify client/index.js -o static/bundle.js
```

Now we can build the client application with the following command:

```
npm run build-client
```

Lastly, let's make our project build and test overtime and start it. For this, add the `prestart` property inside the `scripts` property containing the following command, to build and test our application:

```
npm run build-client && npm test
```

If you follow these instructions correctly, you should end up with a `package.json` file as follows:

```
{
  "name": "web_chat",
  "version": "1.0.0",
  "description": "Web chat application",
  "main": "src/index.js",
  "scripts": {
    "prestart": "npm run build-client && npm test",
    "start": "node src/index.js",
    "test": "mocha tests/*test.js",
    "build-client": "browserify client/index.js -o static/bundle.js"
  },
  "author": "Erich Oliveira",
  "license": "ISC",
  "dependencies": {
    "express": "^4.15.2",
    "ioredis": "^2.5.0",
    "rx": "^4.1.0",
    "socket.io": "^1.7.3",
    "socket.io-client": "^1.7.3"
  },
  "devDependencies": {
    "browserify": "^14.1.0",
    "mocha": "^3.2.0"
  }
}
```

Now we can run our application using the following command:

```
npm start
```

You will see this printed in your console, showing your application bundled, your tests passing, and your application running:

```
[bash-3.2$ npm start

> web_chat@1.0.0 prestart /Users/ericholiveira/dev/workspace/web_chat
> npm run build-client && npm test


> web_chat@1.0.0 build-client /Users/ericholiveira/dev/workspace/web_chat
> browserify client/index.js -o static/bundle.js


> web_chat@1.0.0 test /Users/ericholiveira/dev/workspace/web_chat
> mocha tests/*test.js


  Block user Test
    ✓ Must not receive message from blocked user

  Command Test
    ✓ Must support roll_a_dice command
    ✓ Must support echo command
    ✓ Must send a message if the action is not supported

  Listen to message Test
    ✓ Must listen to messages sent to me
    ✓ Must listen to messages sent to all
    ✓ Must not listen to messages sent to others

  Send Message Test
    ✓ Must support sending a message
    ✓ Must support broadcast message


  9 passing (34ms)


> web_chat@1.0.0 start /Users/ericholiveira/dev/workspace/web_chat
> node src/index.js

Server listening on port 3000
```

Now that we have completed the build of our application, we are ready to implement our client, and we are going to start with the communication with the server.

Connecting to the server application

We are going to use WebSockets to connect with the server through the `socket.io-client`. On the server we modeled, connections and requests as observable objects and we will do the same on the client, To do so, open the `connection.js` file inside the `client` folder, and import the modules that we are going to use:

```
var Rx = require('rx');
var io = require('socket.io-client');
```

So far we have only imported the `rx` module, which we will use to create the observables, and the `socket.io-client`, which we will use to start the connection.

 We will not use ES6 on the client, to avoid the extra step of transpiling it to ES5 and making it work on all major browsers.

Now we need to connect to the server. As we are running on port 3000, we can do this with this code:

```
var socket = io('http://localhost:3000');
```

We only can start to send messages after the connection is established; for this reason, we need observables to listen to `connect` and `disconnect` events:

```
var connectionObservable = Rx.Observable.fromEvent(socket,'connect');
var disconnectObservable = Rx.Observable.fromEvent(socket,'disconnect');
```

In this file we need a way to send data to the server and to listen to data from the server; for this reason we are going to export two functions.

The first exposed function is to send data to the server, and we are going to call it `addSender`; it has the following signature:

```
addSender(observable);
```

It receives only one mandatory parameter:

- `observable`: An `observable` object whose events are going to be propagated to the server

It will have the following implementation:

```
function(observable){
    connectionObservable
            .flatMap(observable)
            .takeUntil(disconnectObservable)
            .map(function(data){
                return JSON.stringify(data);
            })
            .subscribe(function(data){
                socket.emit('request',data);
            });
}
```

The implementation is pretty straightforward; as we can only send messages after the connection is established, we are going to start with the `connectionObservable`, and use the `flatMap()` operator, so, after the connection is established it will start to propagate the data that we want to send to the server.

We also need to stop sending messages to the server if the socket disconnects, and, for this reason, we add the `takeUntil()` operator to stop the observable if a disconnection happens.

We are going to send data to the server as JSON strings; for this reason we need to map each data to a JSON string using the `JSON.stringify` function.

In the final step, we subscribe to the created observable and use `socket.emit` to send data to the server.

 To keep the code and example simple, we will not handle reconnection in our application.

The other method we need to expose must be used to listen to incoming messages from our server; we are going to call it `listen`, and it will have the following signature:

```
listen(event);
```

It receives only one mandatory parameter:

- `event`: It is a string containing the event name of incoming messages from the server

It will have the following implementation:

```
function(event){
    var eventObservable = Rx.Observable.fromEvent(socket,event);
    return connectionObservable
        .flatMap(eventObservable)
        .takeUntil(disconnectObservable);
}
```

In this function, we first create an `Observable` from the given event name in the socket, and we apply the same trick that we used in the previous method to listen to data only while we are connected, starting with the `connectionObservable` and stopping with the `disconnectObservable`.

These two methods are the only thing we need to start sending and receiving WebSocket messages.

If you followed the instructions correctly, you will end up with a file as follows:

```
var Rx = require('rx');
var io = require('socket.io-client');
var socket = io('http://localhost:3000');

var connectionObservable = Rx.Observable.fromEvent(socket,'connect');
var disconnectObservable = Rx.Observable.fromEvent(socket,'disconnect');

module.exports = {
    addSender:function(observable){
        connectionObservable
            .flatMap(observable)
            .takeUntil(disconnectObservable)
            .map(function(data){
                return JSON.stringify(data);
            })
            .subscribe(function(data){
                socket.emit('request',data);
            });
    },
    listen:function(event){
        var eventObservable = Rx.Observable.fromEvent(socket,event);
        return connectionObservable
            .flatMap(eventObservable)
```

```
        .takeUntil(disconnectObservable);
    }
};
```

Using RxJS to manage user input

Now we must implement the observables to listen to user input; they are going to be used to send messages to the server.

Let's implement the events.js file inside the client folder.

The first thing to do is to use the RxJS module:

```
var Rx = require('rx');
```

We want to send the user messages every time the user hits the **Send message** button or when the user hits enter in the message box.

For this reason, we need two observables, the first to trigger when the user clicks on the **Send message** button:

```
var sendPressedObservable = Rx.Observable
    .fromEvent(document.getElementById('send_message'),'click');
```

This observable is simple and just propagates the event whenever the user clicks on the button.

The second observable will propagate the event whenever the user hits the Enter key in the message box:

```
var enterPressedObservable = Rx.Observable
    .fromEvent(document.getElementById('message_input'),'keypress')
    .filter(function(event){
        var ENTER_KEY_CODE=13;
        return event.keyCode===ENTER_KEY_CODE ||
        event.which===ENTER_KEY_CODE;
    });
```

This observable listens to all events of keys being pressed in the message box; we then filter to propagate only when the key pressed is the *Enter* key.

> The number 13 represents the code for the *Enter* key; we compare it with the properties keyCode and which from the variable event for browser compatibility.

Now we must merge both observables to create an observable that propagates when the Enter key is pressed or when the user hits the **Send message** button.

We can do this with this code:

```
var messageSubmitObservable = sendPressedObservable
    .merge(enterPressedObservable)
```

When the user hits this button, he wants to propagate the content of the message box, and we can implement this with the `map()` operator:

```
.map(function(){
    return document.getElementById('message_input').value;
})
```

There is no reason to propagate data if the value is empty, so we also add a filter to check if it has something to send:

```
.filter(function(message){
    return message !="";
})
```

And for the last, we want to erase the content of the message box when the user sends the message, so we need to add a side effect with the `do()` operator:

```
.do(function(){
    document.getElementById('message_input').value='';
})
```

Now we have an observable that emits data every time a user wants to send a message; this observable has the following code:

```
var messageSubmitObservable = sendPressedObservable
    .merge(enterPressedObservable)
    .map(function(){
        return document.getElementById('message_input').value;
    }).filter(function(message){
        return message !="";
    }).do(function(){
        document.getElementById('message_input').value='';
    });
```

In this file we wanted to map all possible user inputs, so the last thing we need to do is to export this observable, so another file can map the messages and send it to the server:

```
module.exports=messageSubmitObservable;
```

If you followed the instructions correctly, your `events.js` file on the `client` folder will have the following content:

```
var Rx = require('rx');

var sendPressedObservable = Rx.Observable
    .fromEvent(document.getElementById('send_message'),'click');

var enterPressedObservable = Rx.Observable
    .fromEvent(document.getElementById('message_input'),'keypress')
    .filter(function(event){
        var ENTER_KEY_CODE=13;
        return event.keyCode===ENTER_KEY_CODE ||
        event.which===ENTER_KEY_CODE;
    });

var messageSubmitObservable = sendPressedObservable
    .merge(enterPressedObservable)
    .map(function(){
        return document.getElementById('message_input').value;
    }).filter(function(message){
        return message !="";
    }).do(function(){
        document.getElementById('message_input').value='';
    });
module.exports=messageSubmitObservable;
```

Now we must implement a way to send the user messages to the server.

Connecting user interactions and server communication

Now that we have already implemented the observable to listen to user interactions and also a way to communicate with the server, we must now implement three things:

- A way for the user to provide their name
- Send messages to the server when a user wishes
- Show on the screen the incoming messages from the server

To implement this last part of our application that connects the user interactions with the server, we are going to implement the `index.js` file located in the `client` folder.

The first thing to implement this is to require the modules we need:

```
var Rx = require('rx');
var connection = require('./connection');
var events = require('./events');
```

With these three lines of code we require the RxJS module and the connection and events modules. Now we can ask a user for their name, and we will use a prompt for this:

```
var logged = prompt("Please enter your name", "");
```

Now when you run the application and open it in the browser, you will be prompted for your name, as you can see in this screenshot:

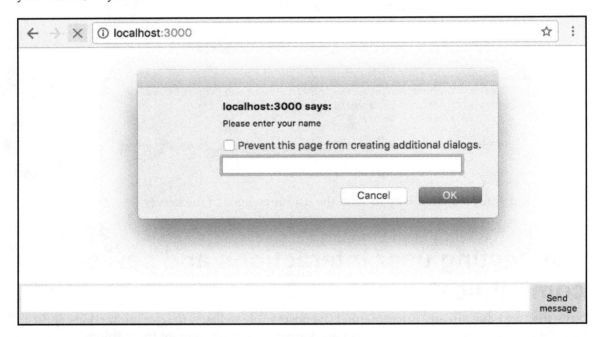

The name you provide is going to be used in the messages.

 To keep the example as simple as possible, we decided to not create any kind of authentication.

Now we need to create the observable of messages for the user.

This can be done with this code:

```
var messagesObservable = events.map(function(value){
    var userName,splittedUserInput,action,content;
    if(value.indexOf('!')===0){
        userName = value.substring(1);
        return {service:'blockUser',blocked:userName,from:logged};
    }
    if(value.indexOf('/')===0){
        splittedUserInput = value.split(' ');
        action = splittedUserInput[0].substring(1);
        content = splittedUserInput.slice(1).join(' ');
        return {
            service:'command',
            action:action,
            content:content,
            from:logged
        };
    }
    if(value.indexOf('@')===0){
        splittedUserInput = value.split(' ');
        userName = splittedUserInput[0].substring(1);
        content = splittedUserInput.slice(1).join(' ');
        return {
            service:'sendMessage',
            to:userName,
            content:content,
            from:logged
        };
    }
    return {service:'sendMessage',content:value,from:logged};
}).merge(
    Rx.Observable.of({service:'listenToMessages',me:logged})
);
```

Here we need to map the user input to the format of messages expected by the server, and we will do this using the `map()` operator; the message can follow one of four different patterns to call different services:

- If the message starts with an exclamation mark (`!`), it is a message to block a user, and the exclamation mark must be followed by the username; we handle this type of message on the first `if()` clause in the function
- If the message starts with a slash (`/`), it is a command message and must be followed by the command; on our server we support two different commands, `echo` and `roll_a_dice`; this is handled by the second `if()` clause

- If the message starts with an at mark (@), it is a private message and must be followed by the `userName` and the message to that user; this is handled in the third `if()` clause
- If none applies, it is a broadcast message.

Besides that we also merge it with an observable containing a single message. This message is used to call the `listenToMessages` method in the server so we can start to listen to messages for this user.

The next step is to use this observable to send messages to the server, and we can do this with the `addSender()` method, as you can see in this code:

```
connection.addSender(messagesObservable);
```

Now we are able to send messages to the server using the input from the user. The next step is to listen to messages from the server and show them on the screen. We can do this with the `listen()` method:

```
connection.listen('message')
    .map(function(message){
            var li = document.createElement("li");
            li.innerText = message.from + ' says to '+
        (message.to || 'everybody')+' : '+message.content;
            return li;
    }).subscribe(function(node){
        document.getElementById("messages").appendChild(node);
    });
```

Here we started to listen to all incoming messages from the server; we then map this messages to a `li` DOM element using the `map()` operator and, finally, we `subscribe` to the observable to show the message on the screen.

If you followed the instructions until this point you end up with an `index.js` file inside the `client` folder as follows:

```
var Rx = require('rx');
var connection = require('./connection');
var events = require('./events');

var logged =  prompt("Please enter your name", "");

var messagesObservable = events.map(function(value){
        var userName,splittedUserInput,action,content;
        if(value.indexOf('!')===0){
            userName = value.substring(1);
            return {service:'blockUser',blocked:userName,from:logged};
```

```
    }
    if(value.indexOf('/')===0){
        splittedUserInput = value.split(' ');
        action = splittedUserInput[0].substring(1);
        content = splittedUserInput.slice(1).join(' ');
        return {
            service:'command',
            action:action,
            content:content,
            from:logged
        };
    }
    if(value.indexOf('@')===0){
        splittedUserInput = value.split(' ');
        userName = splittedUserInput[0].substring(1);
        content = splittedUserInput.slice(1).join(' ');
        return {
            service:'sendMessage',
            to:userName,
            content:content,
            from:logged
        };
    }
    return {service:'sendMessage',content:value,from:logged};
}).merge(
    Rx.Observable.of({service:'listenToMessages',me:logged})
);

connection.addSender(messagesObservable);

connection.listen('message')
  .map(function(message){
    var li = document.createElement("li");
     li.innerText = message.from + ' says to '+
    (message.to || 'everybody')+' : '+message.content;
    return li;
  })
  .subscribe(function(node){
    document.getElementById("messages").appendChild(node);
  });
```

Congratulations! This means you have your first application using functional reactive programming with RxJS. You already can send and receive messages using it.

If you run your application and open it in your browser, you can start to use it, and it will work as follows:

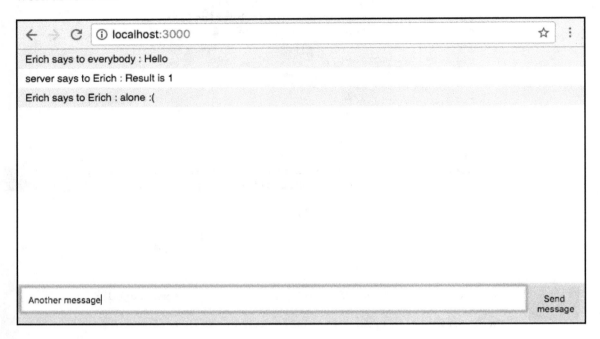

You can even open two browsers to see it run:

Now that we have finished the basics of the web chat, we will see two new interesting tricks that we can do using RxJS in a client application. The first will be to listen to events that are not available out of the box like a triple click, and see how it would be a lot more difficult to implement without functional reactive programming, and also how we can have performance improvements batching changes to the DOM.

Improving interaction with RxJS

One of the advantages of using functional reactive programming, is that it makes it easier to create rich user interfaces, creating new ways for the users to interact with your website. There are several ways to do this.

In this section, we are going to create an Easter egg for our web chat application. Easter eggs are hidden functionalities that can be accessed following one or more steps.

Our Easter egg will be accessed using a triple click in the message box. Every time a given user does a triple click in the message box we are going to fill the message box with the /roll_a_dice command.

 In this section, I want to show you how you can easily create new ways for your user to interact with your application using functional reactive programming. I've chosen to use a triple click, because it is not a standard interaction, and I will compare the code needed to implement it, with and without functional reactive programming.

First let's see how we can implement it using RxJS.

To implement it, let's change the events.js file inside the client folder, and, in the end of the file, let's create an Observable to listen to clicks in the message box; we can do this with the following code:

```
Rx.Observable
    .fromEvent(document.getElementById('message_input'),'click')
```

Now we need to detect consecutive clicks in the message box in a certain timeframe; let's say a triple click must occur in at most 800 milliseconds. To implement this, we could use the bufferWithTime() operator, but what if our user clicks really fast. There is no reason for the application to wait all the time if the user already did three clicks; for this reason, we are going to use the bufferWithTimeOrCount() operator.

Then we need to apply the operator on the Observable:

```
Rx.Observable
    .fromEvent(document.getElementById('message_input'),'click')
    .bufferWithTimeOrCount(800,3)
```

Using this operator, will trigger an event every time a user does three clicks or the given time frame is elapsed after the first click, so we also need to add a filter() to make sure the user completed the three clicks.

It can be done with the following code:

```
Rx.Observable
  .fromEvent(document.getElementById('message_input'),'click')
  .bufferWithTimeOrCount(800,3)
  .filter(function(events){
    return events.length === 3;
  })
```

That's it; this observable triggers an event every time a user does a triple click action in the message box.

Now we need to change the value of the message box with the /roll_a_dice command, and we can do this with a subscription in this Observable:

```
Rx.Observable
    .fromEvent(document.getElementById('message_input'),'click')
    .bufferWithTimeOrCount(800,3)
    .filter(function(events){
        return events.length === 3;
    }).subscribe(function(){
        document.getElementById('message_input').value='/roll_a_dice';
    });
```

If you run this code and test it in your browser, you will see the message box being filled with the /roll_a_dice command every time you do a triple click in it:

Now let's see how we can implement the same behavior without functional reactive programming. The same behavior can be implemented using the following code:

```
var count=0;
var timer;
document.getElementById('message_input').addEventListener("click",function(
){
    count++;
    if(!timer){
        timer = setTimeout(function(){
            count=0;
            timer=null;
        },800);
    }
    if(count===3){
    count=0;
    clearTimeout(timer);
        timer=null;
        document.getElementById('message_input').value='/roll_a_dice';
    }
});
```

As you can see, it is a lot harder to read. We need to create two variables in another scope, the first to count the number of clicks and check if it is equal to three, and the other to reset the counter after the interval.

We also need to manually start and clear timeouts when using this approach.

Needless to say, it is now a lot harder to understand, read, reuse, maintain, and test.

Batching changes to the DOM

When developing a frontend application, one of the greatest problems for performance is the access to DOM.

Changing or adding nodes in the DOM can have a serious impact on your application's performance.

Using RxJS, we can easily mitigate this problem using buffers to aggregate changes before applying it to the DOM. In our web chat application, every time a user sends a message or you send a message, we need to add a new node in the DOM. Given the nature of our application, we do not expect to receive several messages per second (or the user will not be able to read the messages), but if you were implementing a chart with real-time data, this behavior can quickly become a bottleneck for you.

Here, in this section, we are going to do a minor change to our application so all changes in the DOM are buffered before being applied. I will show this technique as it can be used in several other applications.

In the `index.js` file we have the following code; we use it to listen to incoming data from the server:

```
connection.listen('message')
.subscribe(function(message){
    var node = document.createElement("li");
    var textnode = document.createTextNode(message.from + ' says to
'+(message.to || 'everybody')+' : '+message.content);
    node.appendChild(textnode);
    document.getElementById("messages").appendChild(node);
});
```

In this code, every time a new message arrives from the server we immediately show it in the DOM; to minimize the access to the DOM we could easily buffer the incoming messages from the server for a few milliseconds.

To implement this behavior, we can use the `bufferWithTime()` operator to buffer messages in a 500 milliseconds timeframe. As discussed earlier, given the nature of our application we cannot expect a huge performance gain using it, but, for other applications, we could buffer longer and get more benefits from it.

So the first step is to add the operator:

```
connection.listen('message')
    .bufferWithTime(500)
//keeps with the other operators and subscription
```

The `bufferWithTime()` operator will propagate empty arrays if no message is propagated in the given timeframe, as we do not want to run the subscription. If we did not receive any message we must add a `filter()` after this to check if we received a message. We can do this checking if the length of the array is bigger than 0, as you can see in the following code:

```
connection.listen('message')
    .bufferWithTime(500)
    .filter(function(messages){
        return messages.length > 0;
    })
//keeps with the other operators and subscription
```

Now we must change the function used by the `map()` operator to return a new DOM element containing all messages:

```
    .map(function(messages){
        var li;
        var i=0;
        var fragment = document.createDocumentFragment();
        for(;i<messages.length;i++){
            li = document.createElement("li");
            li.innerText = messages[i].from + ' says to
'+(messages[i].to || 'everybody')+' : '+messages[i].content;
            fragment.appendChild(li);
        }
        return fragment;
    })
//keeps with subscription
```

In our new `map()` function, we create a document fragment to use as the container for all `li` elements containing the messages, and return this fragment.

With this new approach, the browser will not keep calculating styles and layout for every new message, and will batch the changes in a 500 milliseconds timeframe.

The last thing we need to do is to subscribe to the final observable, so we can finally apply the changes to the DOM and show the messages. Our final code will look as follows:

```
connection.listen('message')
    .bufferWithTime(500)
    .filter(function(messages){
        return messages.length > 0;
    })
    .map(function(messages){
        var li;
        var i=0;
        var fragment = document.createDocumentFragment();
        for(;i<messages.length;i++){
            li = document.createElement("li");
            li.innerText = messages[i].from + ' says to '+(messages[i].to
|| 'everybody')+' : '+messages[i].content;
            fragment.appendChild(li);
        }
        return fragment;
    })
    .subscribe(function(node){
        document.getElementById("messages").appendChild(node);
    });
```

If you run the application and try to send some messages, you will see the application running as expected:

 Nowadays a lot of frameworks use different strategies to avoid applying changes to the DOM, as this can lead to a big performance improvement. Here you can see how you can easily implement this strategy to avoid changes in the DOM with the usage of a few functional reactive programming operators available in RxJS.

Now your `index.js` file should look as follows:

```
var Rx = require('rx');
var connection = require('./connection');
var events = require('./events');

var logged =  prompt("Please enter your name", "");

var messagesObservable = events.map(function(value){
        var userName,splittedUserInput,action,content;
        if(value.indexOf('!')===0){
            userName = value.substring(1);
            return {service:'blockUser',blocked:userName,from:logged};
        }
        if(value.indexOf('/')===0){
            splittedUserInput = value.split(' ');
            action = splittedUserInput[0].substring(1);
            content = splittedUserInput.slice(1).join(' ');
            return {
                service:'command',
                action:action,
                content:content,
                from:logged
            };
```

```
        }
        if(value.indexOf('@')===0){
            splittedUserInput = value.split(' ');
            userName = splittedUserInput[0].substring(1);
            content = splittedUserInput.slice(1).join(' ');
            return {
                service:'sendMessage',
                to:userName,
                content:content,
                from:logged
            };
        }
        return {service:'sendMessage',content:value,from:logged};
    }).merge(
        Rx.Observable.of({service:'listenToMessages',me:logged})
    );

connection.addSender(messagesObservable);

connection.listen('message')
    .bufferWithTime(500)
    .filter(function(messages){
        return messages.length > 0;
    })
    .map(function(messages){
        var li;
        var i=0;
        var fragment = document.createDocumentFragment();
        for(;i<messages.length;i++){
            li = document.createElement("li");
            li.innerText = messages[i].from + ' says to '+
                (messages[i].to || 'everybody')+' : '+messages[i].content;
            fragment.appendChild(li);
        }
        return fragment;
    })
    .subscribe(function(node){
        document.getElementById("messages").appendChild(node);
    });
```

Testing the application

There are several ways that you could create tests for your application; one of the possible options is to create unit tests for your application.

If we decided to create unit tests for our client application, we would need a way to mock the connection with our servers; this would involve creating a new (and slightly complex) build for our tests.

We could also create end to end tests, to test the whole flow of a user. Doing this would probably involve using some external tool to run our tests in the context of a browser and automatize the user input. This would also involve an extra step of running a tool such as **Selenium** or **CasperJS**.

There are several books on the different ways you can test a frontend application. Here I'm choosing to implement the simplest solution, which involves creating a page for the test using mocha as explained in Chapter 7, *Something is Wrong - Testing and Dealing with Errors*.

To do this, let's create a page called `index_test.html` inside the `static` folder; this page will be a copy of the `index.html` page, but it will contain the tests of our application. It is going to be based on the test HTML file from Chapter 7, *Something is Wrong - Testing and Dealing with Errors*.

Paste this content into the page:

```
<html>
<head>
    <meta charset="utf-8">
    <title>Tests</title>
    <link href="https://cdn.rawgit.com/mochajs/mocha/2.2.5/mocha.css"
rel="stylesheet" />
</head>
<body>
<div id="mocha"></div>
<div style="display:none">
    <ul id="messages"></ul>
    <div class="message_container">
        <input id="message_input"/><button id="send_message">Send
message</button>
    </div>
</div>
<script src="https://cdn.rawgit.com/mochajs/mocha/2.2.5/mocha.js"></script>
<script
src="https://cdnjs.cloudflare.com/ajax/libs/chai/3.5.0/chai.min.js"></scrip
t>
<script>
    window.prompt=function(){
        return "Erich";
    };
</script>
<script src="/bundle.js"></script>
```

```
<script>
    mocha.setup('bdd');
    var assert = chai.assert;
    describe('Web chat test', function() {
        // Your test goes here
    });
    mocha.run();
</script>
</body>
</html>
```

This page contains the mocha and chai libraries and the mocha div used to run the tests. As we decided to keep our code as simple as possible and test the whole user flow, we need the HTML elements used to create the observables for the application (the message box, the send button, and the container for all messages); we are placing them inside a div hidden div, so it won't be shown on the screen.

As we do not want to pop a screen asking for the username, we also override the default prompt function, to always return the same name; this name will be used by the logged user.

Finally, we have the script block containing all tests run by mocha.

The first test we are going to implement is for public messages; a given user must be able to send public messages, and it must be placed inside the ul element.

This will be our first test:

```
it('should send and receive public messages', function(done) {
    setTimeout(function(){
        document.getElementById("message_input").value = "hello";
        document.getElementById("send_message").click();
        setTimeout(function(){
            assert.equal(document
                .getElementById("messages").children.length,1);
            assert.equal(document
                .getElementById("messages").children[0].innerText,
                "Erich says to everybody : hello"
            );
            done();
        },500);
    },100);
});
```

In this test, we are first running a `setTimeout()` to wait for the connection to be available (we are waiting `100` milliseconds, which should be enough), and then we fill the message box with a message to force a click of the **send** button. We wait again a few milliseconds for the message to be delivered and check the content of the `<ul>` element, to see if it contains the message. We finally end our tests, calling the `done()` function.

To test our application, we need to have everything running, so, after saving this file, start your application and open it in your browser on this address: `http://localhost:3000/index_test.html`.

You can see your test passing in this screen:

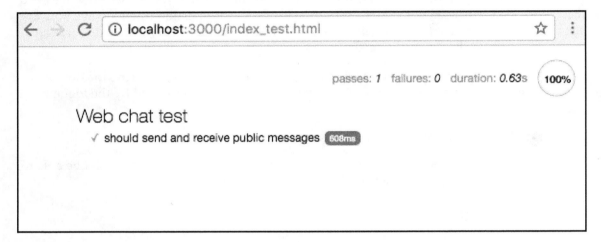

We want to make our tests independent and, for this reason, we are going to add a `beforeEach` hook to clean up the HTML elements before each test:

```
beforeEach(function(){
    document.getElementById("message_input").value = "";
    document.getElementById("messages").innerHTML = "";
});
```

All the other tests follow the same pattern as the first test.

On the second test, we will check for private messages:

```
it('should send and receive private messages', function(done) {
        setTimeout(function(){
            document.getElementById("message_input").value = "@Erich
hello";
            document.getElementById("send_message").click();
```

```
            setTimeout(function(){
assert.equal(document.getElementById("messages").children.length,1);
                    assert.equal(
document.getElementById("messages").children[0].innerText,
                        "Erich says to Erich : hello"
                );
                done();
            },500);
        },100);
});
```

The only differences between this test and the first are the messages sent and received.

In the third test, we will see if the roll_a_dice command works:

```
it('should support roll_a_dice command', function(done) {
        setTimeout(function(){
            document.getElementById("message_input").value =
"/roll_a_dice";
            document.getElementById("send_message").click();
            setTimeout(function(){
                assert.equal(document
                    .getElementById("messages").children.length,1);
                assert.equal(
                    /server says to Erich : Result is [1-6]/.test(
                        document.getElementById("messages")
                        .children[0].innerText ),true );
                done();
            },500);
        },100);
});
```

Here we use a Regex to check the content of the file, as the number returned by the service can be any between 1 and 6.

The last test checks if the echo command works as expected:

```
it('should support echo command', function(done) {
        setTimeout(function(){
            document.getElementById("message_input").value = "/echo hello";
            document.getElementById("send_message").click();
            setTimeout(function(){
                assert.equal(document
                    .getElementById("messages").children.length,1);
                assert.equal(document
                    .getElementById("messages").children[0].innerText,
                    "server says to Erich : hello"
                );
```

```
                done();
            },500);
        },100);
    });
```

If you followed this correctly, you can run the tests in your browser and see a screen like this one:

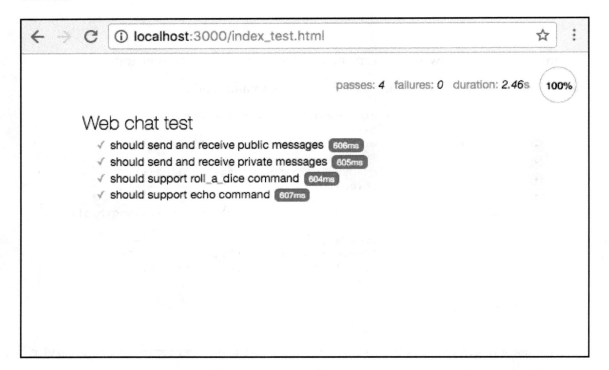

The final code for your tests looks as follows:

```
<html>
<head>
    <meta charset="utf-8">
    <title>Tests</title>
    <link href="https://cdn.rawgit.com/mochajs/mocha/2.2.5/mocha.css"
rel="stylesheet" />
</head>
<body>
<div id="mocha"></div>
<div style="display:none">
    <ul id="messages"></ul>
    <div class="message_container">
```

```
                <input id="message_input"/><button id="send_message">Send
message</button>
        </div>
</div>
<script src="https://cdn.rawgit.com/mochajs/mocha/2.2.5/mocha.js"></script>
<script
src="https://cdnjs.cloudflare.com/ajax/libs/chai/3.5.0/chai.min.js"></scrip
t>
<script>
    window.prompt=function(){
        return "Erich";
    };
</script>
<script src="/bundle.js"></script>
<script>
    mocha.setup('bdd');
    var assert = chai.assert;
    beforeEach(function(){
        document.getElementById("message_input").value = "";
        document.getElementById("messages").innerHTML = "";
    });
    describe('Web chat test', function() {
        it('should send and receive public messages', function(done) {
            setTimeout(function(){
                document.getElementById("message_input").value = "hello";
                document.getElementById("send_message").click();
                setTimeout(function(){
                    assert.equal(document
                        .getElementById("messages").children.length,1);
                    assert.equal(document
.getElementById("messages").children[0].innerText,
                        "Erich says to everybody : hello"
                    );

                    done();
                },500);
            },100);
        });
        it('should send and receive private messages', function(done) {
            setTimeout(function(){
                document.getElementById("message_input").value = "@Erich
hello";
                document.getElementById("send_message").click();
                setTimeout(function(){
                    assert.equal(document
                        .getElementById("messages").children.length,1);
                    assert.equal(document
```

```
                .getElementById("messages").children[0].innerText,
                            "Erich says to Erich : hello"
                    );
                    done();
                },500);
            },100);
        });
        it('should support roll_a_dice command', function(done) {
            setTimeout(function(){
                document.getElementById("message_input").value =
"/roll_a_dice";
                document.getElementById("send_message").click();
                setTimeout(function(){
                    assert.equal(document
                        .getElementById("messages").children.length,1);
                    assert.equal(
                        /server says to Erich : Result is [1-6]/.test(
                            document.getElementById("messages")
                            .children[0].innerText ), true );
                        done();
                    },500);
            },100);
        });
        it('should support echo command', function(done) {
            setTimeout(function(){
                document.getElementById("message_input").value =
                    "/echo hello";
                document.getElementById("send_message").click();
                setTimeout(function(){
                    assert.equal(document
.getElementById("messages").children.length,1);
                    assert.equal(document
.getElementById("messages").children[0].innerText,
                            "server says to Erich : hello"
                    );
                    done();
                },500);
            },100);
        });
    });
    mocha.run();
</script>
</body>
</html>
```

Congratulations! With this test we finished our project using functional reactive programming Now you have mastered RxJS and are ready to use it in your own projects.

As a last exercise, you can try to improve the tests in this application or create new interactions with it.

Summary

In this chapter, we created the last part of our project using functional reactive programming; here we used a lot of the knowledge from the other parts of this book, such as using functional reactive programming in the browser, creating observables from user inputs, using several different operators, modeling messages and connections as observables, subscribing to an observable, buffering data from an observable to process it in batch, and creating simple tests for the frontend application.

We did not use all of the knowledge we learned throughout this book, because it is hard to find a sample application which uses everything, and while keeping it simple enough to use as an example inside a book.

Keep in mind that this knowledge is important and can be used in other programs in your day to day work.

Index

Z